Programming
Interviews

for
dummies®
A Wiley Brand

Programming Interviews

by John Sonmez and Eric Butow

A Wiley Brand

Programming Interviews For Dummies®

Published by: **John Wiley & Sons, Inc.,** 111 River Street, Hoboken, NJ 07030-5774, www.wiley.com

Copyright © 2020 by John Wiley & Sons, Inc., Hoboken, New Jersey

Published simultaneously in Canada

Contents at a Glance

Table of Contents

Introduction

Kudos to you for entering the programming job market. Maybe you're a newly minted programmer looking for your first job, or you're an experienced programmer who wants (or needs) to find a new job. No matter your situation, this book is here to help you do one thing — find the job where you can work happily ever after . . . or at least reasonably so.

Having a résumé and cover letter is just the start of your journey. You need to know what kind of job you want, what kind of company you want to work for, and where you want to work. What's more, these days you may be able to work at home at least part of the time, and you have to take that into consideration, too.

When you've finished writing down (or typing) your list of potential companies you hope to work for, you have to tailor your résumé and cover letter to each one. Then, if you're patient, your journey will start in earnest and the company will ask you for an interview. Though it's impossible to know your chances for success, you're reading this book because you want to succeed.

About This Book

The purpose of *Programming Interviews For Dummies* is straightforward: give you all the information you need so you have the best chance at landing a new programming job. But as you can see from the size of the book, getting your new job is easier said than done.

We help you every step of the way, starting with how to create a résumé and cover letter that stand out, how to network with others, how to ace your tests and interviews, and then how to negotiate effectively so that the company will give you the pay and benefits package you deserve.

This book isn't about how to pass your coding tests, so you'll find only a few brief coding examples in this book. Instead, we recommend several books and websites that give you all the coding examples and practice you need to ace that part of your interview. We also provide programming concept examples that you can apply in any programming language, so you don't have to worry about having to learn a new language to understand what we're talking about.

You'll find a couple of conventions in this book that you should be aware of:

>> Bold text means that you're meant to type the text just as it appears in the book. The exception is when you're working through a steps list: Because each step is bold, the text to type is not bold.

>> Web addresses and programming code appear in monofont. If you're reading a digital version of this book on a device connected to the Internet, note that you can click the web address to visit that website, like this: www.dummies.com.

How This Book Is Organized

We've organized chapters in this book into five parts, and each chapter is arranged into sections that talk about different aspects of the chapter's main subject. Though this book is written sequentially so you can read it all the way through if you want, you don't have to. You can flip to the appropriate chapter or section and read what you want to learn.

Here's what's in each of the five parts:

Part 1: Finding and Hooking Your Next Employer

This part tells you about how to prepare to interview with employers and also understand what employers are doing to prepare for you. You also learn how being prepared will pay off during your job search. What's more, we show that how you provide value to a company is key to not only getting an interview but also one or (hopefully) more job offers.

Part 2: Preparing for Your Interview

In this part, we help you perform some introspection and decide where you want to work, the size and type of company you want to work for, and most important, what type of programming job you want. Then you learn how to find out what's available and where the jobs are so you can shine up your résumé, the accompanying cover letter, and your social networking profiles, as companies look at all of these items closely.

If a company likes what it sees, you'll get a phone call or an email asking you to answer some questions over the phone. We tell you how to pass this phone screen so you can go to the next level: the in-person interview with one or more company representatives.

Part 3: Everyone's Testing Time

The chapters in this part discuss not just the interview itself but also the kinds of tests you'll be asked to perform to show off your programming prowess. If you don't feel like you're fully up to speed with answering programming and personal questions, you learn how to level up your skills so that you'll ace the interview. You also learn about the types of tests you'll encounter, including data structures, detecting design patterns, sorting algorithms, and solving puzzles.

Part 4: Sealing the Deal

After you've had a successful interview, it's time to play the waiting game. You may or may not get a job offer, and this part tells you how to respond in either case. If you get one or more job offers, you learn how to bring your cards to the table, deal with the company, and negotiate the best deal for you — or walk away if you don't like your offer.

Part 5: The Part of Tens

This wouldn't be a *For Dummies* book if it didn't include the Part of Tens. The chapters in this part contain a number of interesting and useful snippets to help you land your next job (and avoid losing an opportunity): Ten Ways to Stand Out, Ten Non-Technical Questions You May Be Asked, Ten Reasons Your Résumé Will End Up in the Round File, and Ten Resources for Information and More.

Foolish Assumptions

When we wrote this book, it was easy for us to assume that you're looking for a job. Beyond that, we assumed the following:

>> You have at least some programming experience in one or more languages such as C++, Python, or JavaScript.

» You're looking for a new programming job with a company and you don't want to work as a freelancer or start your own business.

» You'll do whatever it takes to get the skills you need both in programming and human interaction to get the job you want.

» Even if you don't get the job you want, you'll keep at it until you succeed.

If our assumptions are correct, then this is the book for you. We're confident that the concepts and tactics used in this book will help you achieve your goals.

Icons Used in This Book

This book is stippled with paragraphs that contain various icons so you know these paragraphs need your attention. Here are what the different icons look like and mean.

The Tip icon marks a small piece of expert advice and/or important details you shouldn't miss.

Remember icons mark the information that's especially important for you to know. If you need a refresher about all the good stuff that's in the chapter, just read through all the Remember paragraphs.

This is a programming book, so you'll see some paragraphs that contain technical information (without overwhelming you) and come complete with the Technical Stuff icon.

This book does have some warnings for you. When you see the Warning icon, read the warning text carefully so you understand the effect of what we're saying. The goal of a warning is to save your head from aching.

Beyond the Book

In addition to what you're reading right now, this book also comes with a free, access-anywhere Cheat Sheet that has all the best tips for getting the interview, acing your phone screen and the interview itself, and what you need to know about data types, design patterns, and sorting algorithms. To get this Cheat Sheet, simply go to www.dummies.com and type **Programming Interviews For Dummies** in the Search box.

Where to Go from Here

The first few chapters give you a good overview of what to expect from companies as they look for one or more new programmers to join their teams. We also tell you what to do to make your all-important résumé and cover letter stand out, and also to shape up your social networking profiles to help them shine because interviewers will be looking at them, too.

If the company has contacted you and wants to talk more about the open position over the phone, turn to Chapter 7 to learn what to expect from your phone screen and how to answer questions from the interviewers so they'll want you to come back in person. After you've scheduled your interview, check out Chapter 8 to get ideas about what company interviewers will ask you and how to brush up on your programming and people skills.

Chapters 9 through 12 tell you about the types of problems interviewers ask and how to solve them, but if you're confident in your abilities then you can skim or even skip these chapters. When you shine so brightly to the interview committee that all its members are wearing shades, you can read Chapter 13 to learn what to expect and do if the company offers you the job . . . or not.

Once the company offers you a job, and you haven't negotiated with a company in a long time (or never), read Chapter 14 carefully so you can enter the negotiation meeting at the company with confidence. If you find yourself so popular that you get multiple offers, this chapter tells you how to manage that situation, too.

If you need a checklist of everything you need to have, as well as what you should and shouldn't do, read Chapters 15 through 19. They tell you everything you must do to give yourself the best chance of receiving a job offer from one or (even better) several companies.

1
Finding and Hooking Your Next Employer

Find companies that are hiring programmers and learn how to show your value to a company.

Know how companies are preparing to hire their new programmers so you can tell the interview team how you're the right fit.

Understand how to show interviewers that hiring you will make the company more successful.

Chapter **1**

What Should You Expect?

ongratulations on wading into the river in your knee-high boots to find your awesome programming self a new employer. The river is running fast, so you've got to look sharp to find the right catch.

In this chapter, you start your fishing expedition by understanding the process to get an interview. Next, you learn what your potential employer wants so that you can tailor each résumé you send for each position.

Employers are more likely to respond if you have an application and résumé that has what they are looking for. Once you get a nibble, then you'll start to play the numbers game. That is, it's rare that you'll catch your fish on the first line or even the first ten lines you cast. There are a lot of other programmers fishing at the same time you are, even if you can't see them.

Next, you'll need to put a lot of applications in the water and see what comes up. Some companies will call you and others will email you. And that could lead to phone screens, interviews, and tests. We give you your fly rod, landing nets, wading boots, and all your other gear that *may* lead to a catch — a job offer — and we explain why you may not get one.

Understanding the Interviewing Process Funnel

If you're new to interviewing, or if you haven't interviewed in a while, you may be surprised to find out what happens during the interviewing process. The more prepared you are before the process starts, the better your chances of success. Yes, it's trite, but if you understand why, then you've already taken the first step toward your new work site.

You can think of the interviewing process as a funnel that both you and companies use to find the best match. (If you need to go to the kitchen and get a funnel as a visual reminder, we'll wait.) Employers advertise for a programming job, get a lot of résumés stuffed into the funnel, and then respond to the best résumés that come out the bottom of the funnel, enabling worthy candidates to proceed to the next level.

You're putting a lot of employers at the top of your funnel, too — many are companies you've sent résumés to and some may be companies you've contacted through friends or colleagues who have referred you for an open position, advertised or not.

Before you start the process, you need to make sure you not only have your ducks (or the waterfowl of your choice) in a row, but also that you are careful as you align each duck. Fortunately, your authors are experts in the duck-alignment business, so we provide guidance on how to get your résumé error-free, how to polish your presentation so you aren't nervous or unnerved by an unanticipated question, and how to ace your tests.

REMEMBER

We're going to use the funnel concept in this chapter, too. That is, we'll take all the high-level information you need to know about finding your next employer in this chapter, which is at the top of the funnel. If you want to go down the funnel and concentrate on the topics you need to work on in detail, we tell you which chapters to bookmark for future reading.

Finding Companies That Are Hiring

Searching for companies that are hiring to fill the position you're looking for isn't as easy and straightforward as it may seem. You not only have to know which companies are hiring, but also which companies may be relying on their network of employees to find the right candidate. That means you need to network with those employees — yesterday.

TIP

As recently as 2017, estimates are that between 70 and 85 percent of open positions are filled through professional networks than through job opening advertisements (www.payscale.com/career-news/2017/04/many-jobs-found-networking).

So, what can you do to improve your chances of hooking the company you want to work for?

Meet online

The best place to start to meet other professionals online is the professional social networking site LinkedIn (www.linkedin.com), shown in Figure 1-1. LinkedIn offers the best opportunity for meeting like-minded professionals for two compelling reasons. First, LinkedIn has over 610 million users as of February 8, 2019 (https://expandedramblings.com/index.php/by-the-numbers-a-few-important-linkedin-stats). That being so, employers look at your LinkedIn profile as well as your résumé as they decide if they want to call or email you to set up a phone screen or interview.

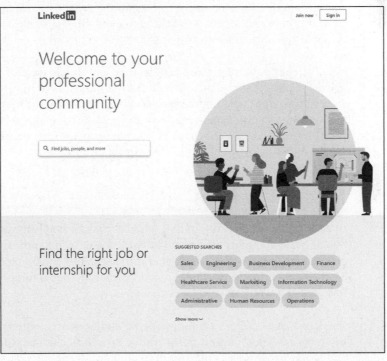

FIGURE 1-1:
Join LinkedIn by clicking Join Now in the upper-right corner of the login page, or sign in by clicking the Sign In button.

Source: www.linkedin.com

Second, you can use LinkedIn to search for the companies you want to work for and see the profiles of the people who work for them. You may get lucky and some of the employees' profiles will include contact information such as an email address you can use to reach out and introduce yourself. If not, then you have two options.

You can send a connection request to the employee. Once connected, members can send and receive messages within LinkedIn for free. When you send a connection request, you should introduce yourself and at least say which LinkedIn user you both have in common to enhance your chances that employee will add you as a connection.

You can also sign up for a LinkedIn Premium account, which is free for 30 days (and $29.99 per month for the Premium Career plan after that). With a LinkedIn Premium account you can send an InMail message to introduce yourself, say what your skills are, and ask for more information about job opportunities.

TIP

When you view the employee's profile, see if the employee belongs to any LinkedIn groups and join those groups. Then you can participate in those groups by starting useful conversations or sending thoughtful responses in other conversations. In time others will respond and the employee will (hopefully) notice that you're a valuable group member and he or she should get to know you better.

If you already have a LinkedIn profile, then you should do a lot of what we suggest above — now. If you don't already have a LinkedIn profile, get one set up and start networking! In either case, craft your LinkedIn profile carefully and follow LinkedIn's suggestions for creating a 100 percent complete profile. Employers will pass you by if they see that your profile isn't 100 percent complete and/or missing crucial information you need to show to get an interview.

Meet in person

In addition to networking online, another way to help improve your chances of hooking the company you want to work for is to network in person. After all, people tend to remember you longer if they can talk to you face to face. Always be on the lookout for professional meetings that are happening in your area and go to as many as you can.

The latest issue of your local newspaper and/or business journal (if there is one) will have a calendar of upcoming events. Your local chamber of commerce website and social networking groups will likely have event calendars, too. The Meetup website (www.meetup.com) shown in Figure 1-2 is also a popular site for finding a list of in-person events about all sorts of topics.

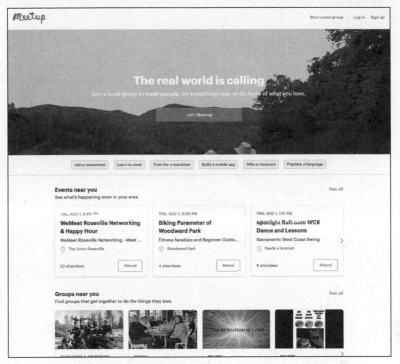

FIGURE 1-2:
Click the Join
Meetup button
to create an
account and find
events that
attract software
developers
like you.

Source: www.meetup.com

TIP

If you go to any networking event, be sure to have business cards ready to hand out after you shake the person's hand. The card should include your name and contact information and list your skills on the back side of the card. If you type **inexpensive business cards** in your favorite search engine, you'll find websites that let you design and order cards in a jiffy, such as the VistaPrint website (www.vistaprint.com) you see in Figure 1-3.

Look at company websites

You should look on the websites of companies that you want to work for in your area and see if you know company employees you can contact. For example, the website may include a blog with the names of people who have written the blog, and you may want to contact the author. The company website may also have job opening posted on one of its pages, such as a Careers page.

Applying to the company directly also has another potential advantage: The company may be using a placement agency as a resource to find new hires. If the company hires you directly, it doesn't have to pay a commission to the placement agency.

FIGURE 1-3:
The VistaPrint website gives you plenty of options to design the right business card for you.

WARNING

Check the company website to see if applications for the open position are only being accepted through a placement agency. If you apply both to the placement agency and to the company directly, it will look to your prospective employer that you're inattentive at best and spamming them at worst — both reasons to put your résumé in the round file.

We get into more detail about searching high and low for companies you want to work for in Chapter 4.

Submitting Your Résumés

Once you've found the companies you want to apply to that have exited the bottom your funnel and landed on your desk, it's time for you to write your résumé and a cover letter to each company.

Each of your résumés and cover letters has to be different because every job description is different. The cover letter and résumé have to show that you can read the description carefully and you have the skills listed in the job requirements.

What's more, each cover letter should introduce yourself and why you're a good fit for the position.

TIP

Consider adding information about ties you have to the company in your cover letter. For example, you can tell people that you met one of their team members (or even the interviewer) at a local event or that you worked with some of the same technologies the company uses in one of your past jobs. Showing a potential interviewer that you've done extra credit work gets you that extra step toward an interview.

It's perfectly okay to take as much time as you need to get your résumé and cover letter right for the job you're applying for, from crafting the layout to a last once-over to ensure you haven't misspelled any words. (You learn more about how to shine up your résumé — and your social media profiles, which are just as important — in Chapter 5.) But what if this extra time getting ready causes you to miss an opportunity, you ask? We cover this eventuality later in this chapter.

If you're still not confident about your skills, don't be shy about looking for résumé and cover letter writing firms in your area. Yes, these firms charge you money, but isn't it worth it to know you have a powerful résumé and cover letter that you can tweak for each job whenever you need them?

REMEMBER

If a company is advertising for several jobs that you qualify for, take care to find out if each job is in a different division of the company. In large companies, one division will send out job applications independent of other divisions in the company. If the company website (or better yet, a contact you know at the company) says the company is smaller, then choose the job you're most interested in because the company will likely consider you for other jobs as well. When you submit multiple résumés and cover letters for different jobs in the same company, that will reek of desperation on your part, and reeking in any situation is a bad thing.

A Company Is Interested! Now What?

With your résumé in the employers' funnels, now you wait to see if yours comes out of the bottom of their funnels so that they can give you a call to the phone number or send you a message to the email address on your résumé or cover letter.

What are the chances you're going to get a call back or an email response? We can tell you that the chances are zero if the contact information on your cover letter and résumé are different. We can also tell you the chances of getting a call back aren't very good if you don't follow up — even if you submitted your résumé late or think you did.

And by *follow up*, we mean that you have to follow up often. When should you start following up? This is where you should contact people in your network who work at the company to get an idea. If you're still not sure, then we recommend waiting one week before calling and/or sending email messages to the human resources (HR) department and/or the manager of the division that's hiring.

Following up aggressively never loses you a job because the company representatives will sense that you want to work for them. It's rare if a company will say outright that it doesn't want to hire you because you're too pushy, and if it does, then that's a company you probably don't want to work for, anyway.

When you get that phone call or email message, the company likely wants to ask you a few follow-up questions to clarify some points or, more likely, wants to schedule a phone screening interview or even an in-person interview. It should go without saying (but we'll say it anyway) that you need to be near your phone and/or your computer so you can take that call or view that email message as quickly as possible so you can respond fast. Companies like that.

TIP

The company representative who calls you will suggest some dates and times for an interview. Have your schedule in your head and be ready to give the company an interview date and time right after the company rep stops talking. Don't pull up the calendar app on your phone while you keep the company rep on the other line waiting while you think about it. If you hem and haw, you've lost the job.

Participating in phone screens

If the company has decided to interview you by phone, which is what companies call a *phone screen*, you need to be aware of what the interviewers may ask of you. For example:

>> You'll be asked technical questions to make sure you can do the job you're applying for.

>> Your personality needs to mesh with other people in the company, so your interviewers will want to know how you behave. Be nice and stay humble. Cockiness or arrogance will tell the interviewers that you won't be a good fit in the company culture.

>> You'll want to show that you're a professional, so answer your questions thoughtfully. Don't lie, don't say anything derogatory, don't brag, and don't try to justify why you don't know something. Any or all of these red flags will be good cause for the interviewers to keep you from reaching the bottom of the company's hiring funnel.

Interviewers may also want to have a meeting using Skype or a different instant messaging app so that they can see you in person as well as give you the ability to solve one or more coding problems on the screen. You learn more about what to do, what not to do, and what to expect in your phone screen in Chapter 7.

Going to in-person interviews

A successful phone screen will likely mean you'll need to schedule an in-person interview. In some cases you'll have only an in-person interview. For example, a company may either be so small that it doesn't do phone interviews, or the company prefers in-person interviews to get a better feel for its candidates.

Depending on the size of the company, you may be interviewing with people from HR as well as with at least one member of the team you'd be working for, or you may be interviewing with the founders of a small or startup company.

Prepare properly

If you can, ask your contacts in the company what the interview process is like and what you should look out for in the interview.

What's more, you may want to ask your friends to participate in mock interview sessions so you can be as ready as possible. Some of those friends can be interviewers and others can be out of view to record your responses so that you can then discuss what to do. These mock sessions may take up part or all of a day, so be sure to stage them where there's plenty of room to operate and allows you to bring in good food to thank your friends. Depending on how good the food is, your friends may be willing to participate in more than one session, and you may even attract one of your connections either in the company or who has interviewed programmers before to participate.

We talk more about how to set up and conduct a mock interview in Chapter 8.

Dress professionally

In an in-person interview, the perception of you as a person is just as powerful (if not more so) as what you can do as a programmer. So dress professionally when you go to your interview. You should dress professionally no matter if you're being interviewed by one person or a panel of interviewers.

TIP

Even if the interview team tells you that you can dress in a T-shirt and flip-flops for the interview, don't do it. Dress professionally. When the interviewers comment that you overdressed for the occasion, it's a perfect opportunity for you to say that you like to present yourself as professionally as possible.

REMEMBER

Think about how you treat someone in uniform as opposed to someone else in casual civilian clothing. You'll treat that person differently even though you may not realize it. If you dress professionally, your interviewers will treat you more professionally and may think you're a cut above the rest.

What's your value?

During the interview, you have to do one thing to get to the next level: communicate your value to the company. Dressing professionally helps demonstrate that you're a professional, but you also need to tell people how you work.

For example, you can talk about a problem you had at a company you worked for and how you worked with other employees both on your team and throughout the company to solve it.

Your interviewers will likely value knowing that you can work independently as well, so let them know you'll do whatever it takes to create solutions that will profit the company. If you can give your interviewers an example of what you did at a previous job to do this, tell your story. Humans are hardwired to tell and respond to stories, and having stories is more memorable and powerful than just saying you've programmed in C++ for ten years.

Being prepared for tests

You may have your programming skills tested during a phone screen, an in-person interview, or both. A company may also schedule you to participate in one or more separate testing sessions after an in-person interview. Testing helps your interviewers understand how you solve programming problems, to wit:

>> What is your thought process to approaching problems?

>> How do you break down a problem?

>> Once you have the problem broken down, how do you craft an elegant solution?

Interviewers don't want to know how you memorize and practice problems, though practicing them is a good idea and you learn how to approach different types of problems later in this book, including:

>> Data structures (Chapter 9)

>> Design patterns (Chapter 10)

>> Sorting (Chapter 11)

>> Solving puzzles (Chapter 12)

Also, in Chapter 8 you learn about online resources you can use to learn how to hone your testing skills.

REMEMBER

Your networking skills will come into play as you prepare for testing, too. You may be able to talk with your connections at the company and other connections both in person and online about the types of problems they've encountered and how they approached the solutions.

When you perform your mock interview sessions, you may want to include programming questions as part of one or more sessions. As you go along, you'll need to talk through how you're solving the problem and why you're solving the problem that way. Speaking out loud as you work on problems — even as you do so online — will force your mind to think through every problem and make you a more confident tester.

Dealing with One or (Better Yet) Multiple Offers

If you've applied to a large number of companies (20 or even more) to maximize your chances of being interviewed, it's possible you may receive one or more offers from companies even as you have other interviews scheduled.

Chapters 13 and 14 tell you about honing your negotiating skills to not only get the highest compensation from the company, but also how to get the most value from your employment, such as retirement plans and how often you can go on leave for any reason. When everyone puts his or her cards face up on the table, you'll need to know when to accept the offer or walk away.

You also learn how to manage your schedule so you can take yourself off the market and get ready to become an employee of your new company.

TIP

You were sure you were going to get an offer from the company you desperately want to work for and it didn't happen. Why not, you cry into the wind? Sometimes the company is keeping a secret: It already has an internal candidate hired or identified but it has to advertise the job because of company policy and/or employment laws. So, you could have a perfect experience interviewing for a company and still not get the job. This is another reason why you should apply (and interview) for as many jobs as possible so you better your chances of landing at least one offer.

Chapter **2**

Knowing How the Company Is Preparing

Just like a sports team selecting players to draft, you can expect every company that wants to interview you will be ready to ask you a lot of questions. The interviewers will also expect that you're prepared, but to prepare you need to know how the company's team is getting ready to evaluate you.

Every company is different, and not just because of the size of the company or the type of product or service the company specializes in. Each business has different needs for the position it's hiring for. Companies have different interviewing processes. And what's more, each company has different levels of experience in conducting interviews.

This chapter starts by telling you about how companies approach an interview. Some may focus on your technical prowess. Others will be more interested in your soft skills, including how you mesh with an existing team, how you communicate with customers, and if you're a good fit with the company culture. You need to know the interview process for each company because in this situation, size matters.

Next, you learn that you can lead the interviews and the interviewers because you have an advantage in the process: You're the one answering the questions.

You can give answers that will make you stand out and unforgettable — beyond dressing professionally as we talk about in the previous chapter.

We conclude this chapter by explaining how all this preparation will pay off for you either in terms of a job offer or making you stronger for your next interview. You may even stand out so well that the company may be forced to hire two people — you and another candidate — because it can't stand the thought of losing you to a competitor.

Learning What Each Company Is Doing

How you approach a company interview depends on the company's environment. After all, trying out for a basketball team requires different skills than those required to try out for a team in football, baseball, chess, or any other sport. (Yes, chess. Ask the International Olympic Committee.)

For example, we've talked to people who have interviewed at Amazon and they report that the environment there is a cutthroat one. That is, Amazon places high value on candidates who are taskmasters and get stuff done — ruthlessly, if necessary. Thus an Amazon interview is an intense one. Google, on the other hand, places a high priority on how smart you are and has a more laid-back interviewing process.

Smaller companies, which are those that can have as few as 100 employees depending on the industry (www.fundera.com/blog/sba-definition-of-small-business), as well as startup companies, have different needs than larger ones.

Gathering information about smaller business and startup needs

When you interview at a smaller company, it'll likely have fewer employees and not as much bureaucracy to deal with. For example, a smaller company may not have a formal human resources (HR) department and may only have one person (or even an external consultant) handling HR duties.

So, you may find yourself being interviewed by the head of the department that's hiring or the person within a department who's either volunteered or been assigned to interview candidates. Since smaller companies have hired employees before, they may already have a set interview process they've developed over the years.

Just because a company is smaller doesn't mean it's in a big rush to hire someone. The time it takes to decide on someone, especially because a new hire has a bigger impact on the entire company since it's smaller, could mean you won't get a response as quickly as you expect.

It's also possible that the smaller company doesn't have a formal interview policy and you'll be talking with one or more interviewers who have little to no interviewing experience. Instead, the interviewers may think of some questions they know they need answers to and ask impromptu questions based on your answers and how they feel the interview is going.

This is especially true at startup companies, which usually have fewer (perhaps much fewer) than 100 employees. You may have an interview with the only one or two programmers on staff and/or the founders of the company. A startup is moving fast because it needs to spend money fast and is on a tight timeline to get one or more of its hot new products shipped quickly.

This being so, the startup company is on one mission: to find the best programmers it can find to meet its deadline and get that big customer, the next round of investor funding, or both. If you can show the startup's interviewers that you not only know the technologies the company needs but also can hit the ground running, don't be surprised if you're offered a job at the conclusion of your interview.

If you're going to interview at a startup company, you should bookmark this page and read Chapter 14 first just in case you're hired on the spot and you need to know how to negotiate fair compensation for your services.

Navigating the involved hiring process at bigger companies

Bigger companies have HR departments, though it's highly unlikely any of them are run by Catbert from the *Dilbert* comic strip. The people who run HR departments follow specific requirements to conduct themselves and the process, but they also understand the legal requirements involved in hiring people. This highly defined hiring process means you should expect a lengthy interview process.

It also means it'll be more likely that you'll talk with more seasoned interviewers and/or they'll follow specific scripts to ensure that the company not only gets the information it needs, but also protects itself from any potential legal exposure.

Yes, once again this is a situation where the networking prowess you learn about in the previous chapter comes into play. If you don't have any connections at the company, try to add some on LinkedIn. You should also try to attend in-person meetings through Meetup or other social networking groups where developers who work at large companies gather. Press the flesh at these meetings so you can pick up crucial information about what the interview process is like at the company you've applied to work for.

TIP

When you scroll down the Meetup home page (www.meetup.com), you'll find a section of categories, one of the first of which is the Tech category. Click the Tech thumbnail image to open the Explore Tech page. Meetup automatically finds your current location and lists groups within 50 miles of your current city (see Figure 2-1). Click a group name to learn more about that group and when it meets.

FIGURE 2-1:
Scroll down the Explore Tech page on the Meetup website to view all the Meetup tech groups near you.

Source: www.meetup.com

TIP

Many big companies have books written about them and how they operate such as *The Everything Store* by Brad Stone (Little, Brown and Company), which is a book about Amazon. If you can find one or more books about a company that will give you insights into how the company thinks and works, that's one more tool you can use as you prepare for your interview.

Preparing for the interviewers you'll meet

Your networking efforts may lead to a connection with one or more interviewers you'll see at the interview, and so you may get some hints as to what to expect during the interview, what the interviewer likes, and, more important, what the interviewer hates. You'll also encounter experienced interviewers, especially from HR, who know what general questions to ask programmers based on past experience.

But you'll also likely find that in many large companies, many interviews are managed by the team that wants to hire a new programmer. And many of the interviewers from that team, especially the ones who are programmers, don't do much interviewing for the simple reason that it's not their primary job.

It's certainly possible the interviewers may be as nervous as you are, if not more so. You should expect that everyone in the company who will interview you will do just as much research about you as you will about the company and the interview process.

The first logical thing interviewers will do is look at your résumé. If they're impressed enough by what they read, they'll type your name in Google (or their favorite search engine) and see what results come up. They'll find your online presence on social media and possibly links to other sites that contain your name. For example, if the interviewer finds that you write a blog and/or you participate in LinkedIn groups about technologies the company uses, that will enhance your standing before you step into the interview room.

TIP

We don't mind if you bookmark this page so you can read Chapter 15 for ten ways you can stand out when an interviewer looks you up online. Go ahead, we'll wait.

Leading Your Interview

During the interview, it is important to take a leadership role, that is, speak with the interviewers in a personable manner and respond to the interviewers' questions in such a way that you steer the interview in your preferred direction — where you highlight your strengths and value to the company.

It is also important to understand the different personality types you might encounter during your interview so that you can respond to each differently. When you go through mock interviews before your real one (nope, we don't think doing so is an option and tell you all about how to conduct one in Chapter 8), you should practice recognizing different personality types and responding to them by leading your interview.

So how you do respond to different personality types?

> >> If any of the interviewers appears nervous, you can set that person at ease by asking the interviewer some personal questions such as how he or she likes working at the company. By creating a personal connection, you'll help put both you and the interviewer at ease.
>
> >> Interviewers may feel that their positions are threatened if you come on board for reasons only the interviewers know. Instead of challenging the interviewers if they become cocky or egotistical, disarm them by giving them some praise about their skills, experience, and recognition.
>
> >> You can also disarm interviewers who are being rude by controlling your emotions. Be respectful toward them and be sure to give them some praise for their work as well.

REMEMBER

These are not the only types of interviewers you may encounter, so when you get together with your friends to talk about conducting the mock interview, don't forget to discuss what personality each mock interviewer will have so you can be prepared to deal effectively with different personalities and keep leading the interview.

Leadership in an interview can also involve talking about hard problems instead of easy ones. For example, if an interviewer asks you about a problem that you had to solve, don't talk about a simple problem that you fixed quickly and easily. Instead, talk about the problem that required you to work with (or even lead) team members, the long hours you and others on your team put in to get the problem fixed, what you learned from the experience, and the positive results.

This approach will help the interviewers like you because it shows that you can work with a team, that you're capable of working on your own, and that you'll do whatever it takes to solve a problem. That is, you'll show the interviewers leadership skills.

Finding out how the interviewer is approaching the interview

One or more interviewers may think his or her role is to ask you only technical questions. Some answers to those questions may be only a few words, like the responses to questions about when something in history happened that you had to answer in grade school.

You may not know the answers to some technical questions because you haven't memorized (or your brain can't bring up) the answer or the questions won't highlight your strengths. In this case, you should steer the conversation by providing answers that highlight your experiences with similar technologies and how you used them to provide value at a company you worked for in the past.

For example, an interviewer might ask you what base class all classes derive from in C#. You could give a one-word answer — System.Object — which would technically be correct. However, it's much better to talk about why they derive from System.Object and to mention that even value types derive from that base class. You could also talk about the functionality that all classes get because they derive from System.Object. The point is, you want to take opportunities to steer the interview in the direction that is going to highlight your knowledge and strengths.

Other interviewers, especially one or more who have non-technical backgrounds, will likely focus on getting to know you and finding out if you'll be a good cultural fit at the company.

For example, an interviewer may ask, "How do you feel about doing work that isn't quite in your job description?" This is the kind of question you should answer by talking about how you wore many hats at your last job or how you've always been interested in marketing as well as software development.

What's more, it's easy to banter back and forth, but it's also important to add stories about how you worked within teams, the role each team member had, the technologies you used to create projects, and how you helped the team succeed in completing projects.

The moral of this story: Telling stories instead of giving rote answers or light banter will give you the chance to shine a little brighter.

Volunteering the right information to make you shine

When you conduct your mock interview, you need to work on finding opportunities to volunteer important information that will make you stand out to the real interviewers. For example:

>> If you've created an iOS and/or Android app that's available in the Apple App Store or Google Play, respectively, let the interviewers know you developed the app and talk about the problem the app solved for people.

>> Talk about a solution you and/or your project team came up with that saved the company a lot of money, helped the company meet a deadline, or even caused a project to finish early.

>> If you're asked why it's been a while since you worked at your last job, tell your interviewers about events that paint you in a positive light. For example, explain that you wanted to go online to learn about a technology you felt you needed more experience with before you entered the job market again. Showing that you're constantly sharpening and mastering skills will impress your interviewers more than a brutally honest answer such as saying you also spent part of the last few months wandering around trying to find yourself.

You don't need to brag about your accomplishments or blurt them out at the beginning of your interview. All you need to do is have these stories at the ready when an interviewer asks you about your experience or a specific question about something in your résumé such as the aforementioned gap between jobs.

What's more, when you're asked about your experiences at companies you worked for in the past, always paint the companies in the best possible light. The companies you worked for were always the best companies, and the people you worked with were the best people. When an interviewer asks you the inevitable follow-up question about why you left, don't lie. If you were fired, say so. But if you felt that you weren't being challenged enough at a company, say so.

WARNING

Never presume that an interviewer is going to know everything about you before the interview starts. For example, interviewers may not even know that you developed an app because they overlooked that information on your LinkedIn profile or couldn't look at your app because they had to do their real job of working on a project instead. Don't miss any opportunity to show that you're a winner.

Showing other ways you're the right fit

Researching the company thoroughly will show your interviewers that you'll also fit right in with the company culture and its objectives. In other words, show that you know the domain in which you're working and that you're prepared to conquer any problem within it. (This concept of a "domain" is not to be confused with the *very* different model portrayed in a famous episode of the *Seinfeld* television show.)

One example is if you're applying for a programming position at a healthcare company. Perhaps you have experience working at a healthcare company in the past, or you previously worked in the medical field before you decided to make a career change and become a programmer. Maybe you worked in the medical field because your mother was a nurse and your sister is a doctor. So, you can mention these experiences to show that you've always been interested in healthcare and in recent years you've been focused on how to make technology work in the healthcare field.

Our point is, if you've continued to study and even build software for the field that the company is invested in, and you can show the time and skills you've invested to learn more about the field the company operates in, you'll show that you just don't want a job — you want to make an investment of your time and skills in the company.

Being Prepared Pays Off

Being prepared in all the ways detailed in this chapter will put you in a far better position than your fellow candidates who will just walk into the interview and think that they can get the job simply based on their technical aptitude.

At best, technical aptitude is about 50 percent of what an interview is all about. The other 50 percent requires soft skills, including:

>> Dressing professionally for the interview.

>> The ability to connect with your interviewers on a personal level.

>> Demonstrating you have technical chops not by reciting information but by telling stories.

>> Explaining to your interviewers how you're flexible by working by yourself and working with a team to help the company succeed.

>> Showing that you understand the industry your company is in and how your experience brings added value to the company.

>> Putting your past experiences and gaps in your employment in a positive light.

Even if you're not offered a job for whatever reason, you can apply your experiences to other job interviews. As you go through each interview, your confidence will increase with each one. Sooner or later, one or more potential companies will notice and decide it doesn't want you to work for its competition.

IN THIS CHAPTER

» Understanding why companies are
   risk-averse

» Helping companies know that hiring
   you is a great move

» Telling companies how you can
   help them

Chapter **3**

Understanding the Investment a Company Makes

A company that hires anyone is making a long-term investment. Hiring a programmer is a particularly valuable investment because a programmer directly affects the products and/or services the company provides.

There's a lot of money contained within the investment of a programmer. The company may have to hire a recruitment or job search firm to advertise for a programmer, and after that programmer is hired, the company has to pay that firm a commission fee. Even if the company hires a programmer using internal resources, including having other programmers as interviewers, the company has to calculate the costs of the programmers' time spent interviewing instead of working on company projects.

After the company hires you, it doesn't just give you a salary — it also gives you benefits such as health insurance and retirement savings plans. And the company has to send payroll and employment taxes to the federal government and to the state the company is located in. What's more, it takes time to train you even if you're really good. It may take a month or longer for you to get up to speed and be as effective as the company needs you to be to make a positive difference for the company.

All of this means that a company is going to be very risk-averse when it hires a new programmer. We start this chapter by explaining why companies are risk-averse and how you can show the company that hiring you will minimize the company's risk. Afterward, we discuss how to tell interviewers what they want to hear: that you'll be a hand-in-glove fit with their culture and that their investment in you will help the company succeed.

Knowing Why Companies Are Risk-Averse

Making an investment in a programmer or any new employee is much like being an investor and making an investment in a company. For example, if we told you that we invested in a hot, new renewable energy company that you needed to invest in too because it will make so much money even Warren Buffett would blush, you'd probably be intrigued *and* skeptical.

You probably won't make any investment of your hard-earned money based just on promised results. You'll want to research the company, the people who run it, and the technologies it uses thoroughly because you want to reduce your risks. Those risks not only include the loss of your money but also the potential legal harm to you if company executives engage in illegal activities. Part of that research is asking us a lot of hard questions to ensure that your investment keeps its promises of low risk and high reward.

Successful companies do the same when interviewing potential new hires, so a company will ask you a lot of questions during the interview process because it knows the risks of hiring a programmer. For example:

>> **Costs to hire a new programmer are high.** They not only include the cost of salary and benefits but also the cost of time needed to train the programmer and the equipment and office supplies needed for the programmer to do her job. And there may also be payments to make to the recruiting firm that found her.

>> **The programmer may prove that he or she doesn't know how to write code despite what his or her résumé says.** It may be that the programmer knows how to fix some bugs and is knowledgeable about technology to pass an interview, but the interviewers weren't as rigorous and/or knowledgeable enough to ask the right questions that would expose the programmer's lack of expertise.

>> **Even if the programmer can code, he or she may write bad code.** Or the programmer has a toxic personality that didn't present itself in the interview.

>> **A company has to keep a programmer engaged and challenged.** If the programmer gets bored, the company runs the risk of having the programmer leave the company for another, sending the company back to square one . . . and there are still deadlines to be met.

In the worst-case scenario, the programmer brings the productivity level of the entire team down — maybe even the entire company. When the programmer is finally terminated, the company has wasted the cost of the training, the cost of time needed to terminate the employee, and the cost to rehire and retrain a new (and hopefully better) programmer.

Different risks for different companies

The type of company you want to join also plays a role in how risk-averse that company is. Even though a larger company doesn't like having to fire anyone because of the lost investment and the need to hire a replacement, it can absorb the costs much easier than a smaller company or a startup. (However, the person who hired the wrong programmer may need to look up some inspirational quotes for getting through hard times.)

A startup or small company is highly dependent on one or, at most, a few key products and/or services that it needs to be produced on time and on budget. Getting a product and/or service out quickly and beating the competition could mean the difference between a large investor investment to grow the company and bankruptcy. The founders or owners are at heightened risk if investors in the company want their money back.

So, when a smaller company hires, it's in a bind: It has to be more careful when hiring a developer to ensure it hires the right one, but it also has to hire someone more quickly. Such time constraints increase the smaller company's risk of making a bad hire, which could jeopardize the company's future. Larger companies, on the other hand, have money in the bank (and, presumably, the confidence of their investors), so they can absorb the costs of firing a bad programmer and finding a better one.

Firing is hard

There's a saying in business to "hire slow and fire fast," but the catch is it's not easy to "fire fast" today. If a company has an experienced human resources (HR) person or department, or is outsourcing HR to an outside company, then the risks to the company from firing someone are minimized because HR experts know the hoops a company has to jump through to legally terminate an employee.

A smaller or startup company that doesn't have a dedicated HR person or department, or one that has inexperienced HR personnel, may not know all the federal and state requirements for firing an employee. The unforeseen risks of company owners or department heads making unintended mistakes could cause lawsuits and filings against the company by various government agencies.

Therefore, smaller companies are especially risk-averse when hiring because the smaller company will have to invest money — which it may struggle to acquire — to hire an experienced HR firm to help the company jump through those hoops and avoid legal risks and even more costs.

Discovering What Companies Are Concerned About

We've talked about the general concerns of different types of companies. But as we know, every company is different, and you have to find out what its specific concerns are about hiring a new programmer.

It's easy enough to ask these sorts of questions at the end of the interview, because when you near the conclusion it's common for an interviewer to ask if you have any questions. In response, you could say, "Hey, I'm just curious, but what are the biggest risks you have in hiring a developer?" If you've established a rapport with your interview team, they'll likely tell you.

TIP

If the interviewers tell you about the risks they're facing, you may want to follow up with some other questions to further inform your ability to assuage the company's concerns, such as:

>> Why are you hiring a new programmer?

>> What is your biggest concern about hiring a programmer?

>> Have you made any bad hires and if you have, what regrets do you have about those hires that you're trying to avoid with this new hire?

Showing How You Can Help the Company

You don't want to inundate your interviewers with questions about their concerns with the company, so you should have some answers already in your pocket when you come to the interview. The best way to learn more about the company's concerns — and be able to then show the company how you can put these concerns to rest — is to network with other employees in the company, as we talk about in Chapter 1.

Your research into the company will inform the types of questions you want to ask current employees either online in a private LinkedIn message or when you ask to talk to a company employee one-on-one during an in-person meeting or mixer. Some questions to ask include:

>> What new hardware and software technologies are you looking into and what challenges is the company facing implementing them?

>> What is the biggest issue facing the company right now and how is the company dealing with it?

>> Why are you hiring a new programmer and how will the new programmer help you overcome these struggles?

Your intelligence-gathering methods will pay off in two ways. First, you can tailor your cover letter and résumé so that they focus on the problem the company is having that you can help solve. Second, you can craft the messages you want to give to the interviewers during your mock interview and then have them at the ready during the real interview. For example, you can say something like, "I know you're working on this new technology and here's the experience I have with it and solving problems in this space. I can help you build and maintain the software and systems you're working on. I can even help the marketing team with communicating the features so customers understand it."

We can feel the Force flowing within you.

Explaining how you can help the team you'll work with

The information you gather about the company can also inform how you're going to improve the team you'll be working with. There are several ways you can communicate that before or even after you submit your cover letter and résumé to the company:

>> **Create a website that shows off your work.** If you're not into web design, there are plenty of free and low-cost website builders, such as Google Sites (`https://sites.google.com`) and Wix (`www.wix.com`; shown in Figure 3-1) that can help you get started. The website doesn't need to be involved — just a place to show screenshots and give brief descriptions of what you did. Don't forget to add information about apps you created or helped develop if you have them, and be sure to add links to your related pages.

>> **Start a programming blog.** One of the pages of your website can be a blog where you can write about programming topics and especially about how you solved problems with teams at another company. (You may need to tweak the parameters a bit to avoid transmitting confidential information from the company you worked for.) There are plenty of blogging platforms such as WordPress (`https://wordpress.org`) and Medium (`https://medium.com`) that help you set up a simple, attractive blog.

FIGURE 3-1: Scroll down the Wix home page to learn more about Wix and get answers to frequently asked questions.

Source: www.wix.com

» **Consider creating a YouTube channel.** Record videos to display on your channel that show people how to program and how to become better programmers. The videos don't have to be very long, either. If you have a good webcam that has 1080p resolution and a good microphone, you can find free and low-cost tools online to record good-quality videos, such as Free2X Webcam Recorder (`www.free2x.com/webcam-recorder`) and Loom (`www.loom.com`; shown in Figure 3-2).

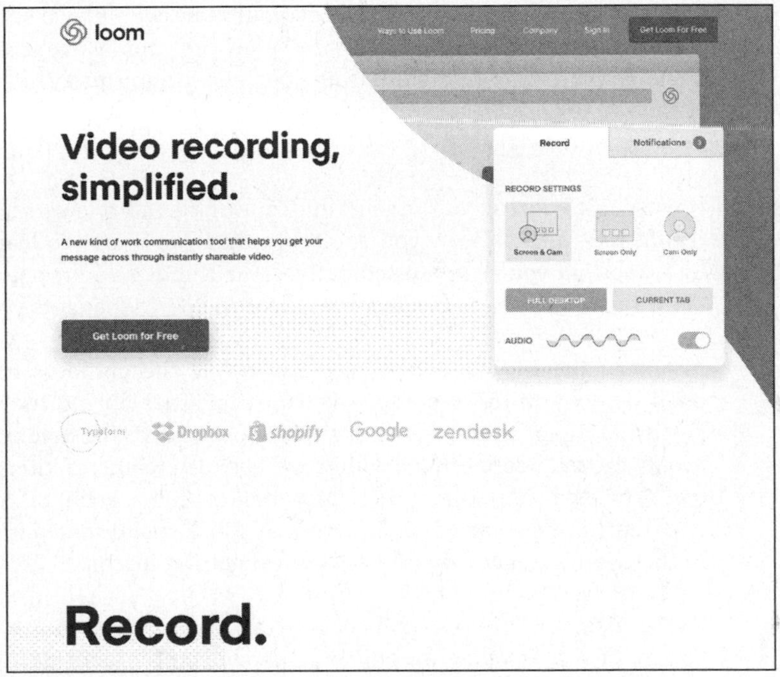
loom
Video recording, simplified.
A new kind of work communication tool that helps you get your message across through instantly shareable video.
Get Loom for Free
Record
Notifications
RECORD SETTINGS
Screen & Cam
Screen Only
Cam Only
FULL DESKTOP
CURRENT TAB
AUDIO
Dropbox
shopify
Google
zendesk
Record.

FIGURE 3-2: Click the Get Loom for Free button to sign up for a Loom account and download the app for free.

Source: `www.loom.com`

TIP

When you maintain a website, blog, and/or YouTube channel, be sure to update them regularly. If you don't, and one or more interviewers notice, you'll need to explain why you haven't been updating your online assets. For example, you could say that you were focused solely on improving one of your apps in response to customer requests so your customers could have the new and improved version as soon as possible.

Demonstrating how you fit into the company culture

If you've read any stories in your LinkedIn news feed or any business websites, you've probably noticed that company culture is a big deal with any business. When you network with company employees and you talk with interviewers, don't forget to ask about and/or pick up on clues on what the culture is like and how it will determine who the interviewers recommend hiring.

For example, there may be people on your team who play a specific online game and they want all team members to be on the same wavelength by playing the same game. If you find out during your networking process that people on the team love to play a specific game and you don't play it, start playing the game and become knowledgeable.

TIP

If you don't know about the game until one of the interviewers asks you if you play it, tell the truth and say you don't, but that you'd love to learn how to play it. Showing that you're interested in the same things as your potential team members and are willing to connect with them could be what gets you the job offer.

Another company may want people who like the outdoors because employees bond by doing a lot of outdoor activities together during the workday, such as participating on sports teams that play on weekends, or holding specific outdoor events to foster connections within and between teams. If interviewers learn that you like being outside, too, then they'll talk with you about all the outdoor activities they have available for employees. If you respond that you're very interested in that, you've taken another step toward getting hired.

WARNING

If you discover that Averagenaut SpaceCo does things you're not interested in doing, such as playing an online game constantly, consider withdrawing your application for the job. Being the odd one out on your team could lead to you finding a new job sooner rather than later. You can spend your valuable time working for Spaceman Spiff's Rocketry where you feel comfortable, and Averagenaut can find another candidate who fits it.

Offering examples that back you up

As part of telling stories about your technical chops during the interview, you need to include examples from your past experiences that show how you learned more about what customers want and how you can best serve them. These experiences can be at different companies and/or your experience creating software on your own (such as smartphone apps).

ERRING ON THE SIDE OF CAUTION

It's a necessity to arrange and participate in a mock interview (with you as the interviewee) as we talk about in Chapter 1 so that you can be as ready for the real interview as you can be. One issue you need to be aware of during the mock interview is that you shouldn't expose yourself as being overconfident in your abilities as a programmer.

For example, you could tell the interviewers that you'll be able to save them 50 percent of their development budget and get projects done months earlier than planned because of your superpowers. Such claims will likely be a big red flag for your interviewers because they won't know if you can follow up on those promises. In other words, you've done what you're trying to avoid — introduced a potential risk.

Instead, keep making the point during the interview that you're going to produce positive results for the company without getting into outlandish specifics. For example, you can tell the interviewers that you'll help make your team better by always providing input, advice, and mentoring when necessary. If you have experience doing that, tell the interviewers where and when you did and what the results were.

Saying that you're a team player will be a big green flag for the interviewers because they'll see you could enhance team productivity and so the company will profit from its investment in you.

If you show that you'll be focused on building the team and know how to do so based on past experience, you'll be able to parlay that knowledge into a better job offer. (We discuss how to improve your negotiating skills in Chapter 14.)

REMEMBER

Even if you're not going to be interacting with customers directly, showing that you've dealt with customers in the past and have at least some knowledge of what they're thinking will only show off more of your value. After all, a programmer who's customer-centric will put out a more usable product that will bring more money and customers to the company.

What kind of examples do you need to come up with? Each example has to show some kind of positive outcome for the company and/or the customer you worked for. Here are some ideas to get you started:

>> How you helped your team improve its productivity and by how much.

>> How one or two times you worked long hours to ensure a product shipped on time . . . or even ahead of time.

>> How your technical skills were key to finishing a software project that made the company money.

>> How you fit into the company culture by participating in different events the company put on so that employees across the company could connect with one another.

>> How you took advantage of company training that turned into an increase in your own productivity, which lifted the productivity of the entire team.

Once you get your brain thinking about examples, you can list those in your notes you bring to your interview. You don't need to write a detailed description in your notes — thinking about examples will (or at least should) jog your memory about what happened during every situation. Then you'll be able to talk about them off the top of your head and enjoy the looks of amazement on your interviewers' faces.

2

Preparing for Your Interview

IN THIS PART . . .

Discover what kind of job you want and learn how to find advertised and unadvertised job openings.

Shine up your résumé and social media profiles to make you stand out to a company's interviewing team.

Prepare for your first phone screen test so you can ace it and qualify for an interview.

Chapter **4**

Searching High and Low for Companies

I f your mother ever complained about you being picky at dinner, your pickiness was good training for finding a job. It's important for you to be picky! After all, where you work isn't just where you spend a lot of your time — your job defines you as a person and your work experiences echo through the rest of your life.

Now that we're done being profound, it's time to search high and low (and near and far and . . .) to find your next job. This chapter starts by telling you how to choose the best method for finding your next programming job. You also learn how to find the best type and size of companies that will give you the best chances of not only of getting a job but also being happy working for your new employer.

Then, you have to be profound yourself and answer a deceptively basic question: What type of job do you want? For example, do you want to work for a company in a specific field such as rocket science or in brain surg — er, healthcare?

Next, you learn how to get the lay of the land locally and beyond if you can't find the job you're looking for that's (reasonably) close to you. After your tour, this chapter ends by telling you about the benefits and challenges of each of the three ways to find jobs: using job search websites, hiring recruitment agencies, and networking with people.

Getting Your Ducks in a Row

It's time to sound the bugle, get your ducks into a row, and snap them to attention. (If you prefer to use cackling geese, we won't judge you.) It's time to send them on their mission of finding you a new programming job at a company you'll love so that you won't have to worry about interviewing again for a good long while.

The mission includes answering a number of questions:

>> Where do you want to work?

>> Where should you work?

>> How do you find the job you want?

>> Should you use job search websites?

>> Should you even look for advertised jobs?

>> Should you go to a recruitment agency to get a job?

Answering all of these questions may seem overwhelming, but as your guides, we'll help you and your flock get closer to the answers by the time you finish reading this chapter.

Deciding Where You Want to Work

The first question about where you want to work doesn't refer to a company. Instead, we're talking about the physical location where you want to work.

Do you want to work only in your local area or in a metropolitan area that's closest to your home? Your current life situation will go a long way toward answering that question. For example, if you're married with a family, you may not want to move. Even if you're single, you may want to stay where you are because you like the life you've built there and other factors, such as the distance between you and your family.

REMEMBER

If you're set on staying put in your city or town, then your ability to do so may be dictated by what programming languages nearby companies use and your flexibility. That is, if companies in or near your area use Java and you program in C++, then you'll have a moment of clarity: Learn Java and have a better chance of staying home, or keep using C++ and either try to find a job that allows you to work remotely — or pack your bags.

Search for a local technology ecosystem

If you're working in an area where there's one large company, you'll likely find a large number of other companies in that same area that help support that large company's systems. For example, if there are one or more large healthcare systems in your town or region, you'll likely find a number of large and small technology companies that provide the critical hardware and software systems needed for the system(s) . . . and they need programmers.

Commute or move?

If working locally isn't a necessity, you have more options to consider. One option may be to work in a different city and commute between your current home and that city because you don't want the hassle and expense of moving closer to where you work.

Before you commit, however, consider the expense of commuting. If you drive, you'll have varying vehicle expenses depending on the price of gasoline and if you have to take your car in for maintenance more often — or for repairs if you have an accident on the road. What's more, if you drive over toll bridges, you have to add the cost of daily tolls or monthly passes offered through services such as the San Francisco Bay Area's FasTrak system.

Commuting will also change how you approach negotiating your salary after you've been offered the job. You may want to find out if the company will compensate you in whole or in part for your driving expenses. (The answer is likely no.) And if you take the train, a ferry, or even a plane to get to work, you'll have to factor in the costs of train, ferry, or plane tickets. (You're right: The answer to the company reimbursing you for these costs is also likely no.)

The costs of moving to another state or even to another country, as exciting an opportunity as that is (unless you're moving to Elbonia), may also prove dauntingly expensive. Moving across the country or across the globe for a new job will affect the questions you ask interviewers. For example, you may ask if the company will help you with moving expenses.

The prospect of moving will also change the way you approach applying for jobs. More specifically, you need to establish a strong relationship with the company and its workers to make sure you and the company are a great fit because you may be living in that other state or country for years to come.

Working remotely

Moving to another location may not even be necessary. If you have the tools to work at home and you can work uninterrupted in your home office, is that something you want to do? And will your desire to work remotely keep you from applying to companies you really want to work for because those companies don't allow remote workers?

REMEMBER

Even if a company allows you to work remotely, it may still require you to attend meetings in person once in a while. If that requires you to drive or even buy a plane ticket, you'll need to add those costs to your list of expenses as you figure out whether working remotely will save you money if cash flow is a high priority.

Figuring out the Size and Type of Company You Want to Work For

When you figure out where you want to work, you need to look at the area and see what the job market is like. If you want to work in a big metropolitan area, you'll have a lot of choices . . . and a lot of competition. The size of the company you want to work for also brings you advantages and disadvantages.

Large companies

Working for a large company means there are plenty of opportunities for advancement, which is good for your résumé if you ever decide to leave or the company decides it's time for "realignment." You may also have more freedom to do other things depending on the culture of the company. For example, Google allows its employees to move to different departments when employees feel they need a change or a challenge. Larger companies tend to be more stable, too.

There's always a catch, and in a very large company you may soon learn that you're going to be limited by bureaucracy. For example, you may not be able to write as much code as fast you want to or can because the product has millions of people in its user base and the company can't afford the media scrutiny (not to mention revenue lost to a competitor) from products that don't work. That being so, the company may only allow you to write small amounts of code and have it reviewed and tested repeatedly.

You may unearth another unpleasant discovery: Some of your team members may not do much for the company because they have very little to do. Some of them may not be monitored that closely, and you might find that they're just coming in to work to basically do little company-related work, pick up a paycheck, and work their side hustle on company time. They may do this because the company's red tape keeps them stuck waiting to get work done, or because they're literally taking advantage of the bureaucracy and doing as little as they can possibly get away with.

Small companies

If you work for a smaller company or a startup, you have a bigger chance to make an impact . . . and a bigger chance to screw up in a way that can damage the company.

In a startup or small company, you may be required to wear many hats. You may find yourself doing many different jobs in the company such as web design, graphic design, project management, marketing, and customer relations. All that work can be very helpful for your career, and you can see that you're making a difference in a company. Another key benefit from wearing all those hats is that you'll probably be given complete freedom (or nearly so) to do everything your way, from choosing what technologies to use to how to market the software.

However, the problem with the term "making a difference" is that it can be connotated negatively as well as positively. If you start finding that you can't do one or more of these additional jobs in addition to the programming you're supposed to be doing, or you've been inspired by George Costanza and modified your desk to take naps under it, your performance will likely suffer. So, eventually you could lose your job not because the company doesn't like you, but because you couldn't get all your work done and the company is going bankrupt.

Given these two choices, you may decide on the Goldilocks approach: Work for a small- to medium-sized company so you can focus on programming and don't have to worry (usually) about the firm's stability.

Wait a minute! you say. *This wasn't helpful at all! I'm not any closer to deciding what to do!* As your Yoda and Obi-Wan, our goal is to make you succeed at what you want to do — not become a Jedi Knight (though that would be cool), but to find the job you want. Only you can decide what path is best for you based on your needs, wants, and circumstances.

TIP

If you're not sure what type of company you want to work for, then bookmark this page, put the book down, and go on a nice walk by yourself. Walking helps stimulate the brain, and if you walk long enough, your brain may finally reveal where you think you should go. More than one walk or other physical activities may be necessary for the answer to pop into your head.

What Type of Job Do You Want?

When you know the type of company you want to work for, you should be as picky about the type of job you want. As we say earlier in this chapter, some of your choices may be dictated by circumstance, but you still have a lot of control over picking the right job for you.

Step one: Technology

Start your journey of discovery by answering questions about the technologies you want to work with:

>> Do you want to work only with new technologies?

>> Do you mind maintaining old systems? You may be surprised by how many programmers keep old code running because their customers don't want to upgrade.

>> Would you like to work on a front-end product where you get to design the interface and the user experience?

>> Do you only want to work on the back end so you can maintain and improve the guts of the software?

>> Do you want to only work with databases?

>> Are you undaunted by working on mission-critical software and/or software that's used by millions of people?

Step two: Environment

Once you figure out which of those jobs you'd like to have, then you have to answer another set of questions to find out what kinds of structure and social exposure you like:

>> Do you want your code vetted and tested thoroughly, which results in slower development times and perhaps requires you to make small improvements constantly?

>> Do you want more structure in your job with set rules and processes?

>> Do you like being in a social environment?

>> Do you want to work from home or come in to work (and leave work) whenever you want?

The answers to these questions will rule out some job opportunities. For example, if you want to work for Spaceman Spiff's Rocketry, you're going to be in a very structured environment where you have to come in every day on time. You'll be in oodles of meetings, and your code will be tested thoroughly because the lives of the astronauts onboard Spaceman Spiff's rockets are in the balance.

Step three: Define your specific role

If you're looking for a specific role within the company, do you know what that role is? If you're not sure, these questions will help you figure it out:

>> What do you think are your areas of expertise?

>> Are you working on some kind of stack or platform?

>> Do you want to create a web application?

>> Do you want to create your desktop applications?

Your answers may tell you that your skill set is lacking to fill the role. The good news is that free education on the web is plentiful so you can make yourself an expert. Once you've planted your flag atop your conquered mountain, you can hone your résumé and cover letter to those jobs, show that you're an expert (as we discuss in Chapter 3), and give yourself a better chance to not only get the job but also a higher salary with it.

Learning What's Available

Now that you have an idea of what technology you want to work with, the work environment you prefer, and the role you want, you have just created a Venn diagram with areas in each of the three circles intersecting in the center, as shown in Figure 4-1. Now you need to fill that magic intersection area with jobs that fit neatly within it.

One good way to find out what's available in your local market is to regularly scan job search sites and recruiter websites to see what's available. Those listings can give you a sense of what's happening in the local job market and what you may need to study to meet those needs.

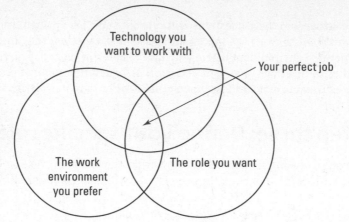

FIGURE 4-1:
The job you're
searching for
is in the
intersection of
technology, work
environment,
and your
preferred role.

(Diagram labels: Technology you want to work with; Your perfect job; The work environment you prefer; The role you want)

Understanding the pros and cons of job search websites

The benefits of job search websites are that they are easy to search, and you can see what jobs are available in your area and what companies want. Job search sites also make it easy to submit your résumé. The biggest drawback is that other programmers are doing the same thing you are. And if you decide to submit your résumé, you have no control over whether it will even be seen, let alone if it'll stand out.

For example, a company may be inundated with several hundred applications from its job posting on a job search website. Even if a human resources (HR) company uses software that allows it to filter applications from the system that don't meet certain criteria, there may still be hundreds of applicants who have passed that first test. The company may then resort to other filters that may or may not whittle down the number of qualified applicants further.

The sheer number of applications works against you because you have no way to stand out, and the company doesn't have enough manpower to manually look through each application. In this case, the company may result to a lottery system and just pick out résumés at random from its database. Or, for all you know, the hiring team may have just printed out all the résumés and had members close their eyes and pick them one by one out of a large box until they reach the number of résumés they want to review.

REMEMBER

Does this mean you shouldn't use job search sites? No. In fact, set up profiles on some of the big job search sites like Indeed (www.indeed.com; shown in Figure 4-2) and Upwork (www.upwork.com). Also search for job search sites on the web to see what other sites you think will give you a better chance of being seen. For example, some job search sites like Hired (https://hired.com) uses its "custom matching software" to match your profile with companies looking for programmers with your skill set.

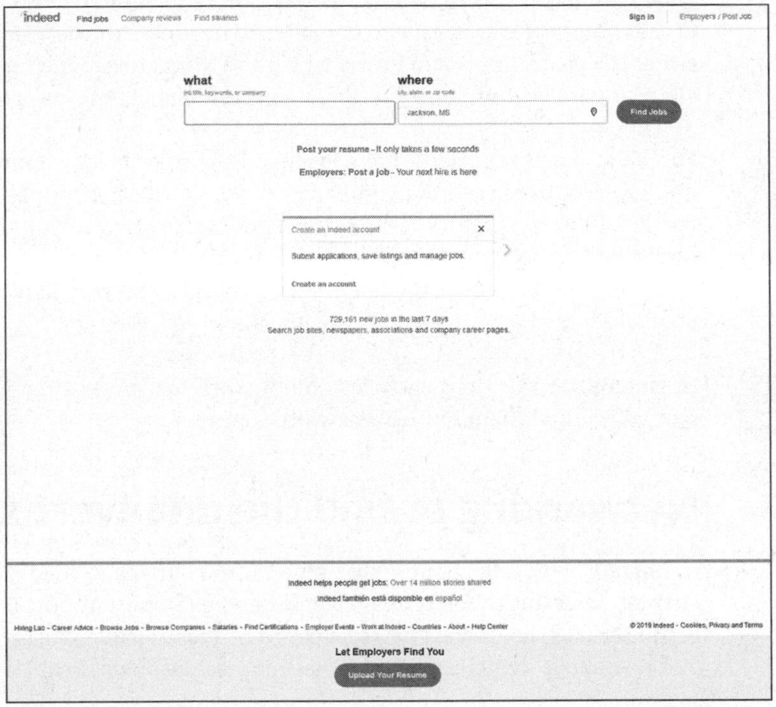

FIGURE 4-2:
The Indeed home page makes it easy for you to search for a job in a specific area quickly.

Source: www.indeed.com

Using and managing recruitment agencies

Some companies may only hire through a recruitment agency, and companies that advertise for opportunities on their websites will include this information in the job description.

Recruitment agencies act akin to financial brokers: If they find a match and the applicant gets hired, they get paid. They're not interested in presenting your credentials in the best way possible; they just want to find a match and hope their candidate gets the job so they make money.

If you approach recruitment agencies and show them that you're a rock star programmer, you may convince one or more of them to work on your behalf to find you a job. Many of the ways to convince a recruitment agency is the same as convincing a company to interview you — show that you're a Jedi Master when it comes to skills and experience, and have website assets that show you're passing on what you know and that you're continually growing and learning.

So, why go to a recruitment agency instead of to the company website directly? One good reason is if you are offered the job, you can negotiate with the agency instead of the company. The agency is compelled to negotiate the best rate possible because either it's paid a lump sum for each hire and wants to get you hired as soon as possible, or because the agency receives a percentage of your pay as commission.

WARNING

You should ask the recruitment agency how it receives commissions and what markup fee it charges the company on top of the hourly pay you receive after you're hired. Be careful that the agency doesn't convince you to take a small pay rate (like $25 per hour) because it says that's all the company you really want to work for will pay while the agency still charges the company $100 per hour for your services.

REMEMBER

In general, recruitment agencies do not work for *you* — they work for the company that hired them to find a new programmer.

Networking to find the unadvertised jobs

In Chapter 1, we talk about networking to find out about unadvertised jobs. In this chapter, we want to focus on strategies and examples of how you can network to *get* those jobs. Let's start by recapping the most visible places to build networks and talk about a couple of places that may not be so obvious.

>> Peruse social networking websites where programmers congregate, like LinkedIn and GitHub.

>> Use business calendars posted in chambers of commerce and business publications to find business meetings where you may find company representatives, especially in industries you want to work in.

>> Use the Meetup.com website to find meetings with other programmers in your town, city, or region.

>> Look for user groups in your city, town, or region that specialize in an operating system and/or programming language you're interested in. You may find these user groups on Meetup.com, LinkedIn, or just through a web search.

>> If you find coding camps advertised on websites like GitHub and Reddit, especially ones that are close to you, sign up and go. The investment will be well worth it because you'll be surrounded wall to wall with programmers.

>> Consider going to conferences for programmers of a specific operating system ecosystem such as Apple's Worldwide Developer Conference or a local

conference about technical issues. You'll find not only a lot of programmers there, but also important people from all sorts of companies who you'll want to talk to.

REMEMBER

It takes time to build both your networking approach and your network of contacts. Just because you think (or were told) you're the Chosen One doesn't mean you don't have to put in the work. It takes time to build your connections just like every other network builder.

Listen and ask first

Before you start networking, *take the time to listen.* (You know it's important when we italicize the words.) As your mother may have told you, you have two ears and one mouth, so listen twice as often as you talk. When you talk to a person, don't just come up to her and say how you can help and if she needs someone to give you a call. If someone did that to you at a networking event, chances are that all you remembered about that person was that you were annoyed by her.

Instead, ask questions about the person you're talking to, listen to his answers, and understand what problems he's facing. For example, if you work as a front-end programmer and the person you're talking to says he's having user experience issues, provide helpful feedback and advice he can use. If you show that you not only know your stuff but also you're willing to share it, he'll remember you in a much more positive light — and be more inclined to keep your business card.

Keep at it

Networking isn't a magic wand, and it may not result in you getting your dream job . . . at least not right away. If your mother told you that you were also stubborn when you were a kid, this is a good opportunity to tell your mom you put that trait to good use.

One method you can use to keep showing your interest in working for a particular company and its programming team is to find blogs written by as many programming team members as you can. Then, follow their blogs and comment on their blogs so that you stay in front of the programmers' minds and build a rapport with them. The same can be said of LinkedIn groups that these programmers frequent and contribute to.

You never know when another programming position will open up at the company, but when it does, don't be surprised if one of the programmers approaches you and tells you that he has a job that would fit squarely in the center of your Venn diagram, and that he and other programmers would be happy to recommend you.

Persistence beats everything else when you want to succeed.

Chapter 5

Shining Up Your Résumé and Social Media Accounts

When you're looking for a job, you're in the image business. Just like any celebrity in any field, you're trying to project the best image of yourself you can to fit the role you want to play. (However, we highly discourage wearing fake hair and/or Spanx shapewear as you work to fill the programming role at a company.)

Your résumé and cover letter give a company its first impression of you. Even if the person (or people) responsible for reviewing résumés likes yours, your image management is not yet complete. Today, companies also look very carefully at applicants' social media profiles not only to see that the experiences on those sites (like LinkedIn) match what's in your résumé, but also to confirm that they don't see anything, such as past inappropriate behavior, that could place your résumé in the "to shred" pile.

In this chapter, we show you how to find yourself online using tools like Google so that you know what your current image is on the web. If you're unpleasantly surprised, we show you how best you can rebrand yourself.

Next, we show you how to clean up the social networking profiles you use (and we mean all of them) so that you don't have anything that screams, "Don't hire me!" to the company. We also remind you that you may need to fill in some gaps in your social media presence, such as adding or fortifying your LinkedIn profile because that's where companies and professionals are online.

When you've finished checking yourself out online and you're ready to write your résumé, we tell you about the best approaches to doing so, including when to write it yourself and when to hire a professional résumé writing service. We tie up this discussion in a bow by reminding you about the information you need to include in your résumé.

Finally, at the end of this chapter, you learn about how to write a powerful cover letter to go with your résumé. Afterall, the cover letter is what the hiring person will read first. We guide you along to make sure you not only add the right information to match the job's description, but also include all the parts of the cover letter you need to make it shine so brightly that said hiring person will need to wear shades to read it.

Finding Out Who You Are Online

As a programmer, you know full well that the Internet is pervasive. And so you know that whether you intended to or not, you have a presence on the web. But you may not know what that presence is and how others perceive you because you've never searched for yourself online. When potential interviewers look you up online, they're going to form a notion of not only your skill set, but also who you are as a person.

Potential interviewers, or anyone else for that matter, can find your information in two ways: using the user's favorite search engine and on social networking profiles. For this chapter, we use Google when we talk about searching for your information on the web since Google has more than 92 percent of search engine market share worldwide as of May 2019 according to StatCounter (http:// gs.statcounter.com/search-engine-market-share).

Googling your name to get your online image

When you go to the Google website (do we really have to say it's at www.google. com?), all you have to do is type your name into the search bar and press Enter. As shown in Figure 5-1, the results page displays all the results of your search. You can expect that if you've sent your résumé to a company, everyone who's looked at it have Googled your name.

What they see on the first page of results is what's going to *pre-suade* them. The term *pre-suasion* was coined by social psychologist Robert Cialdini, a best-selling author who is, as of this writing, the Regents' Professor Emeritus of Psychology and Marketing at Arizona State University.

By pre-suasion, we mean that interviewers will convince themselves from what they see on the first page of search results if they want to hire you or not. An interviewer who has seen your search results and is tasked with screening you on the phone will be excited or skeptical about talking with you based on what she sees. If you reach the interview stage, different interviewers will have their own opinions of you even before you utter your first word.

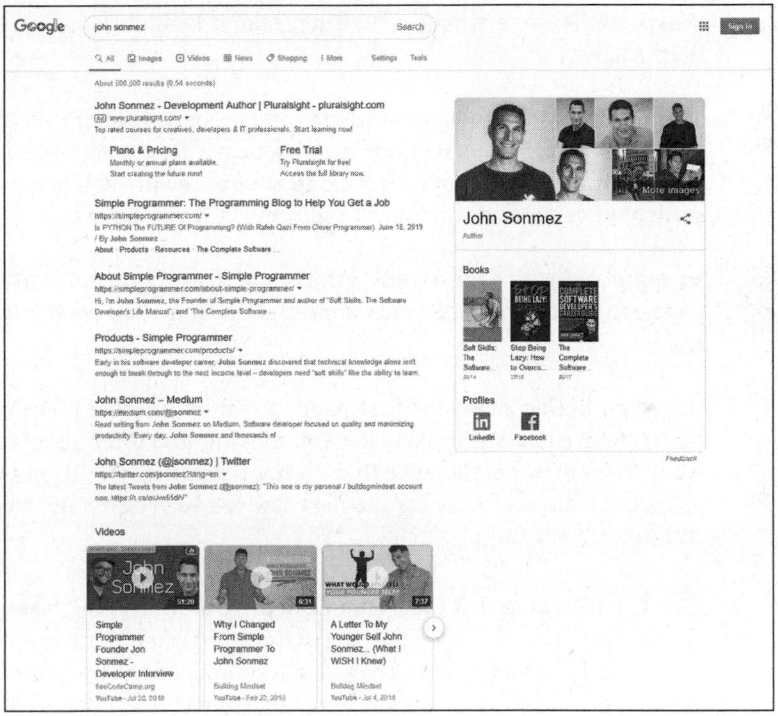

FIGURE 5-1: The results page for author John Sonmez also contains photos and other information like book covers that Google has found.

Source: www.google.com

If you want an in-depth explanation of pre-suasion and how to influence people, pick up two books written by Dr. Cialdini. The first, *Influence: The Psychology of Persuasion* (Harper Business), which was written in 1984, became a classic best seller, and was revised in 2006. The other is *Pre-suasion: A Revolutionary Way to Influence and Persuade* (Simon & Schuster) that was published in 2018. You can view Dr. Cialdini's website at www.robertcialdinibf.com.

Learning how to rebrand yourself

What do you do if the first page of search results about you makes your stomach churn? Start by opening a notes or spreadsheet app or just (gasp!) get out a piece of paper. Then create two columns: one that lists what you want to see on the first page of search results about you, and the other that lists what's showing up on the screen.

When you're done typing or writing, take a look at your list. Do you feel good? Bad? Meh?

This is where your network of friends and perhaps former colleagues can help. Ask them to search for you on Google and get their first reactions to what they're seeing. Getting extra sets of eyes looking at your results will help you get even better control of your image and how to improve it if you have to.

In appreciation of your friends' efforts, we suggest you offer to evaluate their first page of results, too. They may appreciate it, but then we don't really know your friends.

Once you decide that your first page of results needs a makeover, where do you start? Your friends will likely get you moving and offer suggestions whether you want them to or not, because that's what friends do. We'll get you moving, too — block out time every day for the next few weeks (yes, really) to create new online resources. For example:

> **Create a blog that talks about the programming languages you specialize in.** Once you set up the blog, start writing often. For example, you can write tutorial posts about how to solve certain problems you've encountered in your experiences to show companies that you're actively helping others. You can also write your observations and opinions about trends and issues in software development.

> **Record and post videos on your YouTube channel that show you in action programming and solving problems.** (Today you can find excellent webcams for under $100.) What's more, consider showing your face on screen because your viewers and companies like seeing who's giving a presentation.

Just be sure to clean up your face and look and dress professionally so that it looks like you're presenting to a professional audience (such as a group of interviewers).

» **Create an online portfolio website that shows off your best work.** Just search for "portfolio websites free" (without the quotes) in Google or your favorite search engine to find one you like, such as Squarespace (www.squarespace.com) shown in Figure 5-2. Or you can create a full-blown website to show off your website development skills.

» **Have good GitHub and Stack Overflow profiles.** These sites are likely to come up high on Google search results for your name because they're high-profile sites. It takes time to build up these profiles, but the investment may be worth it. Just don't get so carried away with building up your profiles on these sites that it looks like you spend all day on GitHub and Stack Overflow.

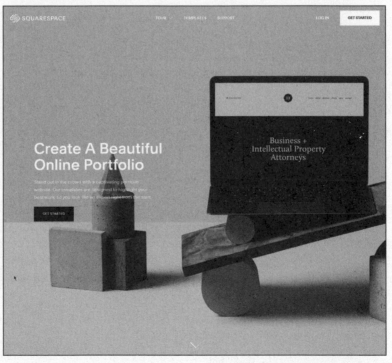

FIGURE 5-2:
Create an online portfolio on the Squarespace portfolio webpage.

Source: www.squarespace.com

You need to remember two things as you create these new resources. The first is to check job postings for programmers and talk to people about open programming positions, which you learn how to do in Chapter 4. (If you haven't looked at that chapter, bookmark this page and read Chapter 4 while we take a coffee break.)

When you know what skills companies are looking for, be sure to include those keywords prominently and frequently in your blog, video descriptions, and/or website. Some examples of keywords include:

>> Big data

>> C#

>> Java

>> Object-oriented programming

>> Polymorphism

>> SQL

>> Visual Studio

The more a search engine sees your keywords, the more likely it is that companies searching for your name and a particular programming forte will find it on that first results page.

WHAT IF YOUR SEARCH RESULTS REVEAL TOO MUCH?

Let's consider the worst-case scenario: Your online search results make you audibly gulp because you can see online that some serious problems in your past, like criminal activity, show up in a search. Your mugshot may also appear in the first page of those results. Not mentioning your past to an interviewer is not an option because interviewers will see that, too, and if you appear as if the situation is no big deal or isn't worth mentioning, then you aren't worth hiring.

Instead, address the issue head on in your cover letter where you talk about the mugshot and/or other past criminal information the company will find it its search. This proactive approach is also an opportunity for you to tell people how your being in trouble led you to a better life. What's more, being up front will show interviewers that you're a human being and that you keep growing from your experiences.

Cleaning Up Your Social Networking Profiles

Social networking profiles are even better at showing — and exposing — who a person is. For example, if you've ever looked at a Facebook or Instagram profile, you can get a feeling for whether someone is arrogant or friendly, their life priorities such as staying in shape or drinking a lot of beer, and what their political leanings are.

What's more, your interviewers will have their *pre-suasions* reinforced or changed based on what they see on your social networking sites. If they find photos of you volunteering to help kids code at your local school, they'll probably like you better. But if they see a lot of photos with you partying every weekend, interviewers may see you as a liability. (If you don't understand why that's bad, then we can't help you no matter how many times you read this book.)

Understanding your visibility online

What's more, an employer can run background checks and hire private investigators to thoroughly investigate your background, and part of those checks include getting access to your public and/or private social networking profiles.

Even if you don't think they can find your private profiles, there's no way for you to know for sure. So, rely on the trite saying "better safe than sorry" and follow our helpful tips for checking and cleaning up your social media profiles before you send out one résumé and cover letter.

Remove some photos, keep others

Delete any photos on all your social media profiles that don't show you in a good light. For example, showing off nice photos of you and your family at a cookout or other event works in your favor. Just make sure you have more photos that show you working in your field in a variety of capacities than photos of you and your cat.

WARNING

You may have heard the truism that anything posted on the Internet is there forever. So, if potential employers find any photos of you even in the recent past that make them physically recoil, you should be up front about those photos in your cover letter as you would with any other experiences during your younger days.

Join LinkedIn and build a consistent profile

Join LinkedIn if you haven't already, and ensure that what's on your résumé matches what's in your LinkedIn profile *exactly*. That is, ensure that the dates in your profile and résumé are consistent. Don't lie about your job titles, such as saying you were the CEO of a company when you were really a freelancer, or you were an employee when you were a contractor.

Once again, always presume the company can find out everything about you. If you're not convinced, take the advice of Mark Twain: "If you tell the truth, you don't have to remember anything."

If you have an existing LinkedIn profile, go through it carefully and cross-check it with your résumé so you don't have any red flags such as a missing job on your LinkedIn profile that's listed on your résumé. Then go through your profile and update it wherever you can. For example, add information about the professional organization you joined recently and replace your headshot with a new one so you look the same way you will when you attend an interview. (A profile photo taken 10 to 15 years ago doesn't work on dating websites, let alone LinkedIn.)

Use social networks properly

People expect you to have more personal information on your Instagram and Facebook profiles. However, on LinkedIn you may have received a message or two in your newsfeed forwarded to you by a LinkedIn contact who didn't quite get the message that LinkedIn is for professional, business-oriented information, not personal stuff.

If you're using LinkedIn to promote something or someone else that isn't related to your job, stop doing it and remove past posts from your profile that aren't professional because (yes, again) presume companies can find it.

TIP

Religion — including theism (or not), computing or device platforms, and programming languages — and politics are two issues you should delete from your profile and not post on LinkedIn. Both topics are polarizing subjects that can form your interviewers' pre-suasions, and even liking another user's post that supports a particular position or candidate can be fatal to your chances for an interview.

Learning what helps get you an interview

Now that you know what won't help you get an interview, what will?

Start by building a complete LinkedIn profile. LinkedIn takes you step by step toward creating a complete profile and will let you know when you've reached the magical 100 percent completion mark. What's more, LinkedIn tells you where your profile is deficient, and occasionally offers advice for making your profile even better. One of the pieces you need to fill out your profile is a photo, and if you're going to be taken seriously by any company, you need to have a professional headshot on LinkedIn. If you don't know how to get one, bookmark this page, read Chapter 15, and we'll be ready to go when you get back.

Next, what do you need to show in all of your online materials to get an interview?

Show you know what you're doing

Competency in one or more programming languages you specialize in is the key that opens the door to an interview room. Earlier in this chapter, we tell you about the various online media you should invest time and a little bit of money to create, such as a blog and a YouTube channel.

But don't stop there: You can create and operate a podcast, self-publish books, ask to speak at conferences, and engage in discussions on social media groups such as those found on LinkedIn.

As you chat online with others, someone may think you're wrong about something and won't be shy about denouncing you. In this case, don't take your ball and go home — it's a valuable opportunity to defend your position . . . or even change it if new information requires it. Companies like to know a prospective employee can not only defend a position like an adult, but also knows when it's time to change it.

Share as often as you can

Share your knowledge with others and don't just tell people how you mentored team members in the last company you worked for. Show how you helped kids in your community learn to code. And if you've spoken at conferences, have videos of you speaking on your YouTube channel to reinforce that you don't just share — you lead.

Keep growing and learning

You also need to tell people in social media posts about what you're reading and what you're learning. These posts can foster discussions where you further show your competence. Later in this chapter, we tell you how to write your cover letter and turn a gap in your employment history into an opportunity to show you're learning.

Removing what can disqualify you in an employer's eyes

The size of the employer you've applied to join may determine what types of information you can have on your social media profiles. Startup and small companies may not be as concerned as larger companies about your questionable choices when you were younger. They may only be interested in your skills and your ability to get their product out fast so that they can secure that next round of funding.

Companies of any size that are more established — that is, have one or more products or services that are bringing in steady revenue — will be more conservative in terms of risk. Established companies have human resources (HR) departments (or an HR company they contract with) and larger companies have their own legal departments.

These companies are well aware of legal liabilities and don't want to hire people who could invite a potential lawsuit because of their political views, religious views, and/or attitudes toward different races and genders. What's more, companies will discriminate because humans are hard-wired to do so.

REMEMBER

Hiring managers or interviewers may look upon you less favorably because of anything they think means you won't be a good fit in their company. Even your age may cause a hiring manager to pass on your résumé and there's no way you'll know if that's true, since in most cases companies either won't contact you or will send you a generic rejection letter.

So, now you know why we've told you that you need to be more conservative with your social networking profiles. You shouldn't hide the fact that you're a human being, but if you follow our guidelines in this section then you'll have a far better chance of getting a phone screen and/or interview. (We're not George Zimmer, so we can't guarantee it.)

Making Your Résumé Stand Out

You have to presume that when you send your résumé and cover letter to a company, your application is going to be one of dozens, if not hundreds, that people responsible for hiring their new programmer have to sift through. So, you have to give those people a reason to read your résumé.

You can't physically make your résumé stand up and dance when it comes out of the envelope — or when reviewers open your PDF-formatted résumé from their websites or email messages — but you can make it stand out.

Finding a professional résumé service versus doing it yourself

We recommend you hire a professional résumé service to write or rewrite your résumé. Period. Full stop.

It's natural to ask if hiring a professional résumé service is expensive. Set aside $300 to $500 for your résumé and cover letter service budget. (You may have to pay more if the service needs to write multiple résumés and cover letters.) Companies that charge in that range will produce a great résumé and cover letter that you can tweak for each job opening and that can lead to better offers and higher pay.

Yes, you can write your résumé yourself instead. The CEO of a company can also learn how to write Python code so that she can do the programming herself and doesn't have to hire you. Do you think a CEO will do that, or will she focus on what she was hired or started her company to do, which is to grow the business?

If your brow is still furrowed, just open Google, type **software developer resume writing service** into the Search box, and look at the list of résumé writing services just for programmers. There are so many of them for a reason.

Now that we've convinced you to use a professional résumé service (we hope), it's time to find the right service for you.

Find a résumé writing service for techies

As you might have guessed, you need to search for a résumé service that's tailored to programmers specifically. The next best option is to find a company that offers résumé services for all sorts of information technology jobs including programmers. Avoid a résumé service that writes primarily for non-technical jobs because it's more likely that company won't understand what information you need in your résumé.

This doesn't mean you're not responsible for providing information to the service as you learn about later in this chapter. But résumé services that know what programmers need in their résumés and how to format them correctly so they get noticed is a requirement, not an option.

Check services out thoroughly

Professional résumé services should have a website that contains a portfolio of past work so you can see how they format résumés and what information is included in each one.

If you can find a technical résumé service locally, excellent (in the way Mr. Burns says it). It's always better to meet someone in person and talk with him and learn if this person is a good fit. But if you can't find someone locally, be sure the website allows you to contact the company online or by phone so you can ask questions.

Don't limit your search to one service or to one writer within a service. Though this isn't a life or death situation, finding the right résumé writer can lead you to a higher quality life for years to come, so be thorough.

REMEMBER

You're not looking for the cheapest service you can find. If you want that, you can just look for résumé examples online, write your résumé yourself, and take your chances.

Canvass your network

You should ask your friends or colleagues to review the résumé writing firms to get their thoughts — and ask if they have any recommendations. If you know a recruiter or can get in touch with one through a friend or colleague to get the recruiter's thoughts, that's the equivalent of having your new program run the first time.

We'll leave it to you to negotiate what the price is for the efforts of your friends and colleagues, but remember that it's all part of the investment. Hey, you may even get brownie points by helping one or more friends who are looking for a résumé service themselves. (Never underestimate the value of brownie points.)

Giving your résumé service the right information

A professional résumé service is not a vending machine. You don't put money into the bill slot and have a résumé tailored just for you come out the bottom slot. The service relies on you to give them information about yourself.

You know the old saying: garbage in, garbage out. If you give your résumé writer garbage, you're going to have a poor résumé no matter what the résumé service does. When you're ready to give them information, here's what to do:

>> Give the service every single piece of data you have from your job history in detail, including all your employment dates and job descriptions. Let them pick out what's important and what's not.

>> Even as you give your service writer everything, be sure to point out what's important to highlight, especially from a technical perspective.

>> Don't forget to proofread each draft of your résumé after you receive it from the service. You need to ensure there aren't any obvious errors like the misspelling of a company name and that the résumé reads well, highlights what you want to show off, and includes all the information you need to make a good impression. Yes, there will be multiple drafts because the service writer wants to get your résumé right just as much as you do.

TIP

Ask your friends and colleagues to look at your résumé drafts and see if they find anything. Yes, we keep prevailing upon them, but we promise we don't hate them (though they may have differing opinions of us). Look at it this way — you can tell them (or surprise them) that you'll pay for a thank-you lunch or dinner after you get your new job and you're making oodles of money.

Advertising what you have to offer

As you read your résumé, ask yourself: Is this résumé effectively advertising what I have to offer to the company? The last three words in that question are the key to getting to the phone screen or interview stage.

Consider your résumé to be like a car advertisement in a magazine. If you saw an ad for a BMW and the ad asked you to buy one of the company's cars because it wants to be the greatest, most profitable car company in the world, would you buy it? Or would you be more inclined to buy if they show you a driver with a beautiful significant other sitting alongside you driving on the open road that tells you subliminally that you could have this lifestyle if you buy a new BMW?

Your résumé should also send a subliminal question to the people at the company reading it: Wouldn't you like to have this software developer working for you who can do all the things you want and more, who's raised the bottom line of companies he's worked at in the past, who's mentored people, and who is a leader in the software development community? If the person reading your résumé is saying "Yes!" in her brain, have your smartphone at the ready to take her phone call or receive her email asking to talk with you.

TIP

If a résumé service tells you that you need an Objectives section in your résumé that tells the company what you want, run, don't walk, away from that service and don't look back. Today, many companies will automatically disqualify you if they find an Objectives section at the top of your résumé because the company is not interested in what you want out of the job and/or career — they're interested in what value you give to the company.

Tailoring your résumé to the job description

After you receive your finished résumé, you need to ensure that it can be easily tailored to a particular job description. Unless fortune smiles on you, like the aforementioned new program running the first time, you're going to send a lot of résumés with cover letters to a lot of companies you think you can help.

That means that every skill you list on your résumé that isn't in the job description is worthless, and you need to take those out. For example, if you're applying for a software developer job that requires the applicant to program in Python, the company won't care if you can program in C++, C#, and Java. That information will show up in the job history section of your résumé, but you need to feature your Python skills and experience prominently and frequently.

TIP

If you have your résumé in a Microsoft Word file, don't keep changing the Word file constantly. Instead, keep that file as your master résumé. When you're ready to tailor it for a new job application, make a copy of the master file and give it a different name. (Logically, this new filename should include the name of the company you're applying to.) Keeping a separate résumé for each job application is a big time-saver if a company asks you to send another copy of your résumé. You should also bring printed copies with you to your interview because you can't presume your interviewers will have a copy with them.

Writing a Cover Letter

You'll know a résumé service is worth researching and investing in if it also offers cover letter writing as part of its résumé development services.

A cover letter is necessary for you to be taken seriously by any company because it introduces you and tells the person reviewing your résumé how you can help her company succeed. A cover letter that gets noticed, which is the one you want to write, fits the job description to a T.

TIP

As with a résumé, keep a master copy of your cover letter that you can then copy, rename, and edit so that it speaks to that company and no one else.

REVIEW YOUR COVER LETTER AS CLOSELY AS YOUR RÉSUMÉ

When you receive a copy of the cover letter along with your résumé from your résumé service, be as thorough reviewing the cover letter as you are with your résumé. Yes, that includes bugging your friends and colleagues — again — but at least you can have them review the cover letter at the same time they review your résumé. You, and everyone who reviews the cover letter, want to say the same thing that the reader at the company will say when he finishes reading the letter: "Wow! You're the perfect match."

Fitting the cover letter to the job description

It's easy to find cover letter templates that you can use, but most people who hire new employees, especially experienced ones, can tell which cover letters are generic and which ones aren't. The generic ones tell the reader about the applicant's experience and what the applicant wants to do.

A résumé service should be able to show samples of how it fits its cover letter to match a job description. In other words, your cover letter is a companion advertising piece that needs to tell how the company will benefit, not what you want from the job and in your career.

To illustrate what a good and bad cover letter looks like, let's start with a sample job description:

> We are currently in 13 professional sports across 46 states and in 8 countries! We offer daily leagues for fantasy football, baseball, basketball, hockey, golf, college football, and college basketball. Our mission is to bring fans closer to the games they love via a unique combination of daily fantasy sports, sports betting, and media platforms. We are currently looking for a Senior and Lead Software Engineer to help establish and lead a team centered around the mission of providing a best-in-class experience for our products and customers.

Now here's an example of a bad cover letter for this position:

> I'm excited to talk to you about how my software development skills can benefit your team and how my experience would make me the best fit for this position.

So, what's wrong with this? The text is generic and feels like a letter that's used for every single cover letter sent to every company. This text is likely copied and pasted into a new document and the only differences between that new document and any other cover letter is the company's name and address.

Here's a much better cover letter to submit for this job posting:

> I'm very excited to talk to you about how I can help build and lead a team centered around bringing fans closer to the games they love, as I'm also an avid fantasy football player myself.

This makes it clear that the applicant is applying for this job in particular because he's restated what the company is looking for specifically and the company's mission. The approach is much more personal so it's much more likely to get a response.

Adding the parts of a cover letter you need

We recommend using the popular four-step AIDA model when you write your cover letter. The acronym *AIDA* stands for Attention, Interest, Desire, and Action. When you follow these steps in order, as illustrated in Figure 5-3, you'll end up with a powerful cover letter that will get a company's attention.

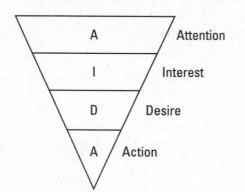

FIGURE 5-3:
The four-step AIDA process starts with Attention and leads the company to Action.

Attention

The first paragraph of your letter should get your reader's attention. There are several ways you can do this:

>> **Tell a story.** Explain what you did in a past experience at another company that not only ties directly into what the company is looking for in the job description, but also how you helped that company succeed. For example, you can say how you helped your team overcome several programming

challenges in Java to finish a project on time and got the company an important client.

>> **Research your company and industry.** Share current research about the
company and the industry. Then show how your programming experience
combined with your industry knowledge can help the company beat its
competition.

>> **Get creative.** The job description and research of the company may prompt
you to get creative. For example, if you're applying to a gaming company, you
may want to say something like, "I want to play," followed by how you not only
played games but have also programmed games in Java in your spare time
that help kids learn how to code.

Interest

If the job description says the company is looking for Java programmers, you can
follow up the attention-getting paragraph noting that you have ten years of Java
programming experience and you can apply what you've learned in your past
experiences to mentor team members and solve the company's most pressing
problems to get projects done.

In other words, you're showing the company the value you can bring to it and how
it'll benefit by having you as a member of the team.

REMEMBER

The interest step is also the place to address any issues readers may have when
they review your résumé. For example, if you have a gap between jobs, state up
front why that happened and how you used that time to better yourself. For example, tell your prospective employer how you used some of that time to read, attend
conferences, and soak up knowledge to get you ready to work for them.

Desire

Now that you have the reader's attention and interest, you need to create desire
for that person to at least put your résumé and cover letter into the "review" pile
so others in the company can determine if you're worthy of at least a phone
screen.

In the desire section of your cover letter, you need to point out the parts of your
résumé that pertain directly to the job description. For example, you can point out
that you've worked for some of the best companies in the world and that you're a
leader in the software development field by giving presentations and writing a
popular blog.

As in a movie or book, you always want to leave the viewers or readers wanting more. So tell them that you feel that you can provide exactly the results the company is looking for and that you can't wait to meet them, tell them more, and show them how you're the right person to solve their problem.

Action

Finally, you need to call the readers to action. That is, tell readers what action to take next, and they're more likely to do so if you tell them directly. For example, say you're available by phone and by email to schedule an appointment to talk more about the position, thank them for their consideration, and that you're looking forward to talking with them further.

Chapter **6**

How Your Experience Affects Your Interview

After reviewers at the company have been impressed by your résumé and your cover letter, and they don't see anything in your social media profiles that make their jaws drop, they'll not only consider interviewing, you but also think about what types of interview questions to ask you.

Your résumé is a microcosm of your work life just like a baseball scorecard is a microcosm of an entire game's activities, so your résumé readers will get an idea of how well you can hit when the game counts.

We've divided the chapter into three parts to help you understand how the company will pitch to you:

» We first explain the differences between a junior and senior developer.

» You then learn what you'll experience during the interview process as a junior or mid-level programmer — meaning someone with little experience or with a few years under his or her belt.

» Finally, we discuss the interview questions you'll get as a senior developer, where experience is the name of the game. If you know you're a senior developer already, you can skip ahead in this chapter to the section, "Playing in the Majors" to get the information you need.

REMEMBER

This chapter presumes you've already learned either from the job description, a recruitment agency, a friend, or a colleague what the company expects as far as experience required for the job. If you only know the programming language the job requires from what you learned at the university (that you graduated from last month), and the company wants ten or more years of programming experience in real-world environments, then you're wasting your time sending a résumé. Instead, look for job descriptions or ask about jobs that don't depend on past experience but rather the right skill set the company can develop.

Qualifying for Senior Status

Always presume the people at the company (especially the programmers) know the difference between a junior and a senior software developer. If you're not sure, here are common responses from people at companies with senior developer positions on the Stack Overflow website (`www.stackoverflowbusiness.com/blog/what-defines-a-senior-developer`). **Senior developers have:**

>> A number of years of programming experience, though that number varies depending on the company.

>> Demonstrated leadership skills.

>> The ability to manage the entire software development life cycle.

>> Supported junior developers and acts as a mentor.

>> Shown they understand and respect not only their own team's environment but also interact well with related teams.

You can read more about these responses, read related articles, and also read several articles about career development for programmers at the Stack Overflow Talent website shown in Figure 6-1.

REMEMBER

No matter if the company is hiring someone it deems to be a junior or senior programmer, the company will protect its investment. That is, the company wants to make sure the person it hires is a capable and good fit for the job no matter what the new hire's experience is. If you're a junior developer, a company wants to invest in you in the long term and help you grow into a senior role. And if you're a senior developer, it wants you to hit the ground running, mesh with the other programmers quickly, and become a leader on the team.

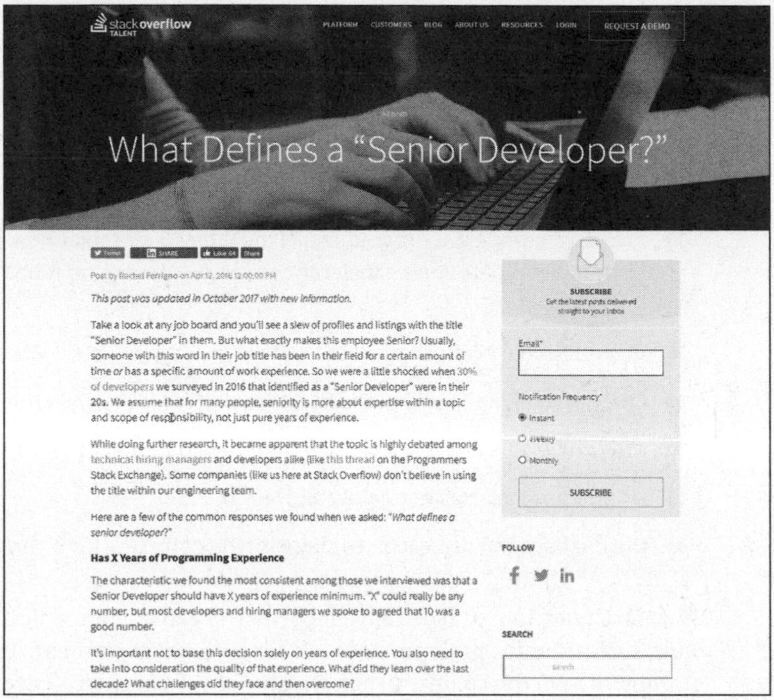

FIGURE 6-1:
Click links in the article to view more information about the topic.

Source: www.stackoverflowbusiness.com

Being More than Just a Junior

The term "junior" has many negative connotations, including being small and secondary, but there are advantages to having junior status. (The classic *Seinfeld* episode, "The Junior Mint" is a case in point.)

In your case, you may fall into one or more junior programmer categories:

» You're someone with no experience as a real-world programmer because you just graduated from school or a coding camp.

» You've spent time working as an intern at one or more companies but not as a salaried employee.

» You're working on your own by taking contract jobs where you can get them or you're writing your own code, such as mobile apps, that you may have on an app store for free — or for a fee.

» You've worked at one or more companies for the past few years and you have some experience delivering code and/or actual products. Some companies call programmers with some experience "mid-level" programmers.

No matter what category you fall into, companies will still see you as a junior programmer and you have to communicate all your other positive qualities to make up for your lack of experience, especially in your cover letter and across your social media profiles. The qualities you communicate have to dovetail closely with what the company wants in an ideal candidate. These qualities include:

>> Are you a competent programmer? (You'd be surprised at how many companies say candidates prove they can't develop software no matter what their résumé says.)

>> Do you have a portfolio of work to show?

>> Can you think and learn quickly?

>> Are you flexible and adaptable in different situations?

>> Do you have the desire to grow and learn?

>> Do you have the dedication to stay with the company for a period of years?

That last question is especially important because companies, especially larger ones, look at junior programmers as a long-term investment. That is, junior programmers save the company money in the short term with lower salaries (at least to start). But over the long term, companies can keep junior programmers around for a while to groom into senior programmers (or a manager). The company may even spend some money to help you develop your skills.

Smaller companies or startups may be more interested in hiring you because they won't have to pay you as much, but they may not be able to invest money in your development (at least not right away). So they'll look you over maybe even more closely than large companies to make sure you can get up to speed quickly and that their investment in you will be worth it.

Show your work

When a company résumé reviewer notes that your work experience is lacking, that person will pay more attention to the education you listed in your résumé. Depending on what that person finds (or not), the company may decide (or have procedures in place) to get more information from you.

If you went to school

You should be prepared to have copies of your schoolwork ready to send to the company representatives if they ask for it, or provide samples to an interview panel.

That schoolwork may not only include completed assignments but also final course grades. Don't be surprised if the company also asks you for information about your instructors so that a company representative can contact them and talk about their impressions of you.

Your grades and feedback from instructors won't only tell the company how talented you are, but also what your work ethic is like. If your work ethic in school wasn't very good, the company will presume that your work ethic at the company won't be very good, either.

If you went to the minors

If you know that a company will have a hard time finding your scholastic information because you decided not to go to a college or university, but instead decided to go straight to the minor leagues out of high school and attend a coding boot-camp or learn on your own, you need to be up front about that in your résumé and especially in your cover letter.

By "up front," we mean you need to focus on pointing to your portfolio of sample projects on your website that people can review. If you can't do that because you've worked with contractors and they won't let you use samples, you need to provide the contractors' information so that the company can contact them for more information.

The right extracurricular activities

When your experience is lacking, companies will also look at your extracurricular activities — and not ones on your social media profiles that show you partying every weekend. Companies want to see that you're spending your free time becoming a better programmer. Company representatives like to know that you're not just developing to have a job, but that programming it's something you enjoy doing and are passionate about.

If you're already writing apps for profit, then you need to mention that you have apps available for download in the Apple App Store and/or Google Play Store and play up both good reviews and how often you're updating the app to serve customers. Showing that you've written code that works and that people are using, and that you're customer-centric will get you much closer to an interview on the phone or in person.

Your extracurricular activities should also show that you're engaged in your community. That can include volunteering at your local school to help tutor kids in coding, running your own group through the Meetup website, and/or participating on a sports team that demonstrates teamwork, discipline, and a good work ethic. If you need more suggestions about how to stand out, bookmark this page and read Chapter 15. We'll be here when you get back.

Character

Qualities such as having a strong work ethic, being disciplined, and being a team player are all part of someone's character. Calvin's dad in the *Calvin and Hobbes* comic strip had it right when he kept pressing his young son to build character even when Calvin (often) didn't appreciate it.

Company reps will look at your character to see what kind of benefits you'll add to the company. (You're right that this is true of any developer, but it's especially true when you don't have much of a portfolio of work to back you up.) When interviewers examine your character, they'll want to see not only someone who's passionate about developing software, but also someone who has a lot of ambition. They want someone who's going to take charge of what she's been put in charge of.

Commitment

Commitment is another aspect of character that warrants special attention by your interview team. We mention earlier that the company is making an investment in you, just like any baseball team is making an investment in a hitter who has tantalizing hints of greatness but needs seasoning (the diplomatic term for a lot of work) before reaching the majors.

Your résumé reviewers will be interested in what you're doing *now* to show that you're reliable without the pressures of a deadline in school or at work. So, here are some ways you can show potential employers that you get things done outside of work:

>> Complete a website and keep it updated.

>> Have a blog and write new posts on a regular basis.

>> Show that your LinkedIn profile is not only complete but also that you write posts and comment in programming groups regularly.

>> Attend regular meetings of programming groups such as those promoted by Meetup and/or regional programming conferences to show you network often.

You may have other activities in your area that you already participate in, such as the aforementioned sports teams. We can hear the gears in your brain turning already.

Point out your activities that highlight your commitment in your cover letter and in your social media profiles so your potential interviewers can find them easily.

Resolve

When we talk about resolve, we're not referring to the carpet cleaner. Interviewers will want to know that you have the resolve to tackle any challenge you find no matter what it is. And they'll test your resolve by giving you programming questions to solve and "soft skills" questions such as how you resolved a conflict with a fellow team member.

Interviewers won't be impressed if you answer a question about resolve by just saying, "Oh, I've handled this before. No problem." A better answer is to say, "You know, no matter what's thrown at me, I'm confident I can figure it out. I'm not worried about it and I'm committed to making sure I get the job done no matter what it takes."

Don't think that resolve means that you have to solve every single problem that comes before you. You learn in Part 3 that you may not be able to solve a programming problem in a set amount of time, or there may be an incident in your past when you weren't able to solve a problem yourself. In those instances, you should include a story about when you weren't able to resolve an issue and how you worked with members of your team to resolve it. Interviewers will be impressed that you can recognize when you need to reach out to others to get the job done.

Don't forget talent

You're interviewing for a programming job, so the interviewers will want to see that you can actually write code during the interview. They'll pitch you fastball programming questions as well as questions to test how you think about problems.

You learn more about the types of questions you'll receive and how best to solve them in Part 3 in this book, but here's a sneak preview of what to expect:

>> If you just got out of college with a computer science degree, the interviewers will throw out computer science questions to see what you learned.

>> Questions about sorting algorithms, data structures, and coding algorithms based on those data structures.

>> How to recognize design patterns. Your interviewers won't expect you to have experience using those design patterns, but they will expect you to recognize some design patterns in code and describe them.

>> Questions about your reasoning skills when you solve problems, such as:

- Why are you doing this?
- Why are you thinking in these terms?
- What is it that's causing you to take these steps to solve this problem?

If you can show your interviewers that you have a clear, rational method of solving problems — especially when you're under the pressure of an interview — this will tell your interviewers that you're a good hitter and that you may belong on their team.

Leave the best for the end credits

All of these values are part of your story as a programmer, and your interviewers want to hear your story in order to get to know you better as a person.

If you're a freshly minted programmer from a college, university, coding camp, or you taught yourself, be ready to tell the story about how you always wanted to become a programmer and why you decided to study the way you did. If you were in school, you may want to explain why you did or didn't join one or more computer-based clubs. You should explain why you did or didn't become an intern at a company. Finally, you should talk about what you've been reading in books and online because you're excited about the latest issues and trends.

However, if you have a few years of experience already and can be considered a mid-level programmer (kind of like a Triple-A player in baseball), you'll want to tell the story of your previous jobs, what you learned from each one, and how your job and your activities outside of work are helping you grow as a software developer.

In sum, the company wants you to answer a simple question: Why should the company hire you, a person who's not that experienced in programming, when they can hire an experienced programmer you're competing with in the interview game? The better story you can tell, one that helps the company understand you better as a person, the better your chances of being picked for the team.

Playing in the Majors

Senior programmers are somewhat of a rarity in the job market and just as with free agent players in major league baseball, your interviewers will judge you differently because you're experienced.

You've handled most if not all of the problems in successfully producing software, so your interviewers' expectations will be higher. They'll want to know that you've demonstrated some leadership skills, helped junior developers, and learn about the different scenarios you've encountered in your career.

Be honest about your career

Interviewers will be most interested in your experience, and that experience likely won't be all good. Maybe you left a company because of personality conflicts that couldn't be solved. Maybe a job became boring and you decided to look for the proverbial greener pastures. You may have been fired or laid off from one or more companies.

One mistake to avoid when you write your résumé, cover letter, and talk with your interviewers is to try to hide any and all bad stuff in your record. Interviewers know you can't hit it out of the park all the time (and if you get the impression that they think you should, there's a big red flag for you), but you still gain experience with each strikeout.

So, don't talk about others or the situations in a bad light, which is likely to put you in a bad light with your interviewers. Instead, talk about what you learned from the situation to make yourself a better programmer, team member, and leader. Your story should show how you progressed from being green and untested to today's seasoned programmer who would be a valuable employee at the company.

Stable or stagnant?

No matter your job history, you're going to field a lot of questions about it. If you've been at your current job for a long time, and now you're looking elsewhere, expect your interviewers to ask questions about your current job, such as:

>> Why didn't you move up into a management role?

>> Why didn't you increase your responsibilities?

>> Are you just happy with the status quo?

The moral of this story is that you need to show that your skills continue to advance over time even if your job title has remained the same. We talk about the skills tests you can expect in the interview later in this chapter.

Ambitious or flighty?

What if your story is that you've been switching jobs too often? That will be a red flag for any company you apply to because the résumé readers may think that you can't fit in with teams and/or you're just not a good programmer, so that's why you keep leaving jobs all the time.

However, interviewers don't know the circumstances of your departures, so if a company contacts you and asks about your work history, you have the opportunity to explain the various reasons for switching jobs. For example, you worked on small-term contracts and the contracts ended to the client's satisfaction. Don't presume that your interviewers know about the contracting world and expect to tell your interviewers how the contracting process works and how you came to find your contracting job(s).

Another reason you may have switched jobs often is because you were wooed away by new opportunities. That could be a big red flag for your potential employer, as it may seem as though you are prone to being swept off your feet by the next suitor who sweet-talks in your ear. You need to tell interviewers why you left for those opportunities, why you believe the company you're interviewing with is a great fit, and why you want to put down roots with the company.

Tell the rest of the story

It's likely you have gaps of time between jobs and your interviewers will want to know all about them. The worst thing you could do is give a simple answer such as, "I just needed a break." Hiding your stories is a good reason for interviewers to end an interview early.

Instead, explain every gap and say what you did during that time. If you decided you needed to take some time off and reenergize your batteries, say you did that and give some details about what you did. If there was a family emergency, say so. If you said you weren't challenged in your job and it was burning you out, say that, too.

TIP

No matter the circumstance, say what you did to become a better programmer during those gaps if you can. In some cases, such as you took care of family issues that required your full attention, you couldn't do that. But if you wanted to finally write that app that you were always working on now and then but could never finish, and you used that time to not only finish it but it's making you money from happy customers, *that's* a good story.

In sum, when you tell your story, tell it completely and in the best way possible.

Education

Speaking of taking time to become a better programmer, interviewers will want to see that you're a lifelong learner. Companies want to see that you're showing some advancement over time.

You don't want to be a senior programmer who never learns anything once you get out of school and draws a blank when interviewers ask what kind of books or blogs you're reading now. If you're relying on what you learned 15 to 20 years ago, you're behind even junior programmers in the competition for the job. (What, you didn't think there were other candidates for the job?)

So, take every opportunity to mention what you're doing to improve your skills — coding skills, interpersonal skills, and leadership skills.

Leadership

Leadership skills are expected from senior developers inside and outside the workplace. In the workplace, you need to be able to voice your ideas in a way that people will not only understand, but also have enough weight for people to take action to get something done or fix a problem.

Workplace leadership also involves working with junior programmers and helping them become better programmers and better members of the team. That type of mentorship can be formal where you have taken a programmer under your wing and now that programmer is considered to be senior level. Or the mentorship can be informal where you give your feedback and encouragement whenever you can. What's more, if you have a problem with a fellow programmer, you know how to resolve that problem discreetly and effectively.

Leadership also requires involvement in the wider community. That is, you should be leading something. The higher the position you're applying for, the more leadership skills and community involvement you need to be involved in. For example, you can do one or more of the following:

>> Lead one or more computing-centric organizations such as those coordinated through the Meetup website.

>> Run an open source project.

>> Participate or volunteer in a code camp for kids, adults, or both.

>> Speak at local or regional programming events.

>> Operate a blog and write new posts often.

>> Maintain a programming podcast and/or a YouTube channel with videos about programming.

If you need more suggestions about how to stand out, you can bookmark this page and read Chapter 15 while we take a break and eat some healthy snacks.

You can also visit the Programming Leadership website shown in Figure 6-2 (https://programmingleadership.podbean.com), listen to podcasts about the topic that are regularly produced by Marcus Blankenship, and find out if that site is a good resource for you.

FIGURE 6-2: The Programming Leadership website offers podcasts about programming leadership.

Source: https://programmingleadership.podbean.com

Flexibility

Workplace leadership also requires you to have skills in other areas. Depending on the job you're applying for, the company you're interviewing with will expect you to wear a number of hats:

>> You should know about databases and how to interact with them.

>> You may need to have some architecture experience as well as the ability to architect the entire solution the company needs — not just implement a solution in code.

>> You should understand cloud technologies, including how to develop applications in the cloud.

>> Understand at least how DevOps works, how a DevOps build is created and deployed, and how a build is put into production.

>> Know what needs to be done when something goes wrong, the build doesn't work, and you need to fix it. (You may have trouble picking just one example of when this happened to you.)

These are all topics that junior developers won't know about or won't be able to do, so as a senior developer you need to be ready to talk about these issues at any time. Even if an interviewer doesn't ask you directly, you may want to talk about how you led your team — especially the junior developers — to use these technologies and fix problems that crossed your path.

Don't forget skills

Companies expect senior-level developers to have other business skills that are important for the company to succeed. Those skills can include:

>> Communication with business analysts and top executives — even the CEO of the company.

>> The ability to communicate between technical and non-technical worlds.

>> Technical writing for technical and/or non-technical audiences.

>> Marketing and/or customer service skills.

If interviewers notice that you worked for a small company, they're going to expect that you have these skills because startups and small companies don't have the resources to hire a large number of people with different skill sets. So, the senior-level developer is the one who gets more responsibilities as well as leadership opportunities.

What's more, if you're applying to work at a startup or small company, then your interviewers (which may be the founders) may expect that you have these leadership skills because there isn't anyone else with your skill set who can do those jobs. (If you show you can do them, you may get a job offer much sooner than you think.)

With all this chatter about non-programming skills, don't think for a second that your interviewers won't ask you about your programming skills; those questions will go deeper. For example, interviewers will expect you to have a higher level of familiarity with design patterns. You should know how to use them and scale them, recognize when design patterns are used at scale, and know how to apply design patterns at scale to build robust code.

TIP

Though it's not necessary to know or have implemented every design pattern there is, you should be able to explain why and how you implemented design patterns in your job. Interviewers will ask about design patterns and other "real world" questions early and often.

You should also presume that you'll not only be tested, but given a more challenging test than a junior programmer to write out on the whiteboard because of those (say it with us) higher expectations.

TIP

Even if you get the same coding problems as a junior developer to write out on a whiteboard, the interviewers are asking you to solve those problems with the expectation that you can pass them. If you can't, then interviewers will question what you've done with all your experience and if you learned anything as a programmer — probably among themselves after they end the interview early and escort you out of the building.

Chapter **7**

Getting Ready for the First Ring

Congratulations! Your résumé and cover letter were a hit, you got a phone call from the company, and you set up an appointment for your phone interview — better known as a phone screen. A phone screen only rarely gets you the job, but it can easily lose you the job.

So, this is a situation where you're playing not to lose. In this chapter, you learn what that means as you prepare for your phone screen. We start by showing you the basics of preparing for your screen and follow that up with a discussion about the types of phone screens you can encounter.

Once you're properly prepared, we finish this chapter by helping you answer both technical and experience questions. We also show you how to code in a live, high-pressure environment; what to do if the company assigns you homework at the end of the call; and how you can avoid disqualifying situations.

Ready to ace your phone screen?

Preparing for Your Phone Screen

When you start preparing for your phone screen, you need to ask the company representative (we'll use rep from now on because we're not the stuffy types) what type of phone screen you're going to have. As you talk on the phone or chat back and forth in an email thread about scheduling the phone screen, you'll have the opportunity to ask for at least an idea of what the phone screen is all about. Some basic questions you should ask include:

>> How long will the phone screen take?

>> Do I need to be in front of a computer with access to the Internet?

>> Do I need to use a specific instant messaging client like Zoom where I'll have to install a web browser plug-in before the call?

>> Will I need to use a webcam for this phone screen?

>> Will this phone screen be about my soft skills, my technical abilities, or both?

>> Will I be solving a coding problem during the phone screen?

If you tell the company rep that you want to be as prepared as possible, you'll likely get some answers. You may also be able to ask some follow-up questions depending on the answers you get.

However, don't be surprised if you don't get all the answers you're looking for, perhaps not even hints, because during the phone screen the interviewer will want to know how well you answer questions on the fly.

WARNING

Don't be pushy about asking questions. If it seems to the company rep talking to you on the phone that you're trying to get all the answers before the test, the rep may decide that you're not a good fit after all and abruptly end the call. Yes, the first call to schedule your phone screen is really your first test.

Prep your space

Speaking of comfort, you should expect the phone screen to take an hour, if not more, even if the company rep you talk to about the phone screen says it'll take less time. And that doesn't include the time you'll take to get ready just before your phone screen, which includes preparing your space.

You should ensure that you're taking the call in a quiet place, not at your local Starbucks. You should also be able to sit in a comfortable chair and have your favorite beverage nearby because you're going to be there for a while. Just don't expect to take bathroom breaks during your call.

If you're going to have a video call, be sure to test your video camera using the software you're using (like Skype) not only to see how you look but also what it looks like around and behind you because your interviewer will see that, too. So, if you have time, tidy up the space that's in view and project a clean image of your work area.

Watch your behavior

We said it once, and we'll say it again: A phone screen isn't where you're going to get your job, but it is where you can lose it, so focus all your energy on answering questions and managing your behavior. If you have to, type or jot down these reminders on a sticky note while you're taking part in the phone screen:

>> Don't come off as overbearing.

>> Don't come off as aggressive.

>> Don't say anything negative about anyone or a previous job.

>> Don't try to knock their socks off.

In sum, just answer the interviewer's questions directly and honestly. You should also smile through the phone. That is, when you talk and smile at the same time, the tone of your voice changes to a happier and friendlier one, and that tells your interviewer that you're engaged and glad to be talking to him.

If you know your voice needs to sound happier — or one of your friends, in a friendly way, says your voice needs to be friendlier — you can learn to do so by reading the wikiHow article, "How to Develop a Friendly Voice" at www.wikihow.com/Develop-a-Friendly-Tone-of-Voice.

Have your friends join in

If you're not confident about passing a phone screen, ask your friends to help you. (They must be pretty annoyed at us by now.) But, just as with a mock interview, a mock phone screen with your friends will be invaluable and your friends will (probably) have a lot of fun trying to flummox you and get you to think. For example, they can come up with both technical and "soft skills" questions such as:

>> Can you show how to solve a basic problem in the programming language we need? (Hopefully one of your friends can supply the problem so you don't know about it before the mock phone screen.)

>> Can you answer other technical questions about the programming language(s) you use on the fly?

>> How do you work with other people?

Certainly your friends can come up with some other questions based on their experiences. If you know one or more people who's worked with the company before, you should ask them if they'll send your friends some test questions. No matter what, don't let your friends tell you the questions ahead of time. The mock phone screen has to be as accurate as possible if you're going to have a chance of succeeding.

Before you start working on the mock phone screen, you also have to know about the types of phone screen you can get. Then ask your friends to prepare for different types of phone screen tests so you can handle any question the company interviewer throws your way. (Yes, indeed, your friends will come up with ideas for compensating them for all their work.)

Reviewing the Type of Phone Screen You May Get

We've talked about being prepared for any type of phone screen because you may not know much about the type of phone screen you'll have ahead of time (though you may get hints). The screens we describe in this section give you the basics, and then we'll go into greater detail later in this chapter.

Basic screen

Some phone screens are very simple. In a basic phone screen, the interviewer isn't evaluating you but instead just getting some additional information from you and recording your answers. Then he'll send those answers to the hiring manager or committee and that person or people will determine if they want to bring you in for an interview.

A basic phone screen doesn't require you to impress the interviewer taking your answers, but you want to ensure that your answers are thorough and well thought out. Sometimes if you give an answer, you may think of a better one later during the phone screen. In this case you can say, "You know what? You asked me a question I think has a better answer, and I'd like to replace my earlier answer with this one if that's okay with you." If you're up front about changing your answer, the interviewer will likely change the answer because she can tell that you're actually thinking.

Another type of basic phone screen is a personality screen. The interviewer will ask you questions that will assess your character traits to see if your personality is best suited for the open position. It's likely the interviewer will use one of several different types of personality tests, so you may receive multiple-choice questions or be presented with two different types of statements and asked which one you agree with most.

One of the most common personality tests is the Myers-Briggs Type Indicator (www.myersbriggs.org), which you've likely heard of when you've heard someone call themselves an INTJ or ENFP or one of those variations. This common test determines personality attributes like extraversion versus introversion, intuition versus sensing, thinking versus feeling, and judging versus perceiving.

Another popular personality test you might encounter is the DiSC Behavior Inventory (https://discinsights.com). It's one of the oldest personality tests and helps determine how strong you score on dominance, influence, steadiness, and compliance. It helps determine a person's professional behavior and work style.

Technical question screen

During a technical question phone screen, the interviewer will ask you a series of technical questions designed to elicit the following information about you:

>> Whether you have specific knowledge about the company's technical activities based on your review of the job description and research of the company.

>> Your understanding of the programming work you'll be doing as part of your job. The interviewer will likely ask you about what you did in some of your past jobs based on what he reads in your résumé.

>> How familiar you are with the programming language the company needs you to know. Don't be surprised if the interviewer asks you about some of your sample work on your website, blog, and/or GitHub account.

You may also be asked some coding questions and asked to answer them over the phone instead of showing live code, which will show that you understand programming concepts and know how to solve problems. For example, the interviewer may ask you, "What is heap and stack in a process?"

TIP

If you want to review a list of 50 phone interview questions you may be asked as well as concise answers to each question, check out the Javarevisited blog post, "Top 50 Programmer Phone Interview Questions with Answers" at https://javarevisited.blogspot.com.

Live coding assignments

Your interviewer may go further by asking you to do one or more coding assignments live during the phone screen. These assignments require you to have an Internet connection and may require you to use an existing instant messaging application such as Skype.

The company may provide you with an email message so you can log into its preferred instant messaging client like Zoom. In the latter case, you'll likely have to install an application on your computer and/or a browser plug-in.

TIP

If you find that you have to have a webcam for your phone screen, then you may want to use your laptop that has a built-in webcam instead. If that's not an option, you can purchase good webcams for less than $100 these days, and you can use it not only for any future interviews but also for creating video tutorials to show your prowess to potential employers, as we talk about in Chapter 5.

With live coding assignments, you may have to share your screen so the interviewer can see what you're doing, or the messaging app will allow a shared space within the app window so that you can type within that area and the interviewer can see everything you're doing. What's more, your interviewer may not tell you how he's going to conduct the test because he wants to see how you adapt to what may likely be an unfamiliar programming environment for you.

Doing live coding under pressure may be old hat or it may be something new. Either way, practice solving different kinds of tests after you've searched on Google for the best interview questions and problems in the programming language you're using. For example, you may need to master solving algorithm problems before you go on to the next problem.

REMEMBER

This practice is worth the time investment because you're playing the long game. That is, if you pass the phone screen, you'll likely be asked to perform coding tests under pressure during the interview, too. Or, if you don't pass the phone screen with this company, you'll be much better prepared to succeed in another company's phone screen and/or interview.

Acing Your Phone Screen

Now that you know about the basics of phone screens, how can you get the information you need not only for a successful mock phone screen but also to pass the real thing? In the sections that follow, we explain the do's and don'ts of acing your phone screen.

Answering basic technical and experience questions

As part of your preparation to answer your interviewer's questions, look at the job description and then fire up Google so you can search for examples of interview questions for different programming languages.

For example, type **best Python interview questions** in Google to bring up a large selection of Python-based interview questions to review and practice answering.

Here are some common Python interview questions you'll likely find in your search:

>> What is PEP 8?

>> How is Python interpreted?

>> How is memory managed in Python?

>> What is a lambda in Python?

>> What are generators in Python?

>> How do you convert a number to a string in Python?

>> What is the use of the split function in Python?

TIP

As you go through the answers, make sure you not only know what the answers are, but also *why* they're the right answers. Don't presume that the interviewer won't ask you to justify any answer you give during the phone screen.

When you answer your questions, speak in an authoritative tone — not at the Eric Cartman level ("Respect my authoritah!"), but don't start your answers by saying, "Well, I kind of," either. Instead, speak confidently and tell your interviewer that you have the experience and the know-how to get the job done. That may lead you to the next step in your phone screen — doing some live coding — so you can show as well as tell.

If you have a GitHub account that includes samples of your work, your interviewer will likely ask you questions about those. Expect your interviewer to look to see if you're on Stack Overflow. It's likely she will review your experience on that site, check your top answers to see how helpful and knowledgeable they are, and see if you have a high reputation. The latter is especially important because on Stack Overflow your reputation is awarded by your programming peers.

Coding live on an instant messaging client

In addition to answering basic technical and experience questions, the interviewer may also give you one or a series of coding assignments to complete during the phone screen. Some of them will be easy, and you should be able to solve those without any trouble. As we discuss earlier in this chapter, you'll get instructions for how to access the instant messaging client from your interviewer so you can log in a few minutes before the start of the test and be ready to go.

The interviewer will tell you what environment to use to perform any live coding with a time limit. For example, you may be asked to share your screen and open Notepad so that you can type in a simple text editor without access to any of your usual shortcuts.

As you're typing, you should also talk about how you're approaching the problem, why you're doing what you're doing, and why your solution works when you're done.

If you're having difficulty solving the problem, tell the interviewer that you're having difficulty and why. The interviewer will likely appreciate that because his goal with live coding assignments is not to have you write perfect pieces of code every time, but to learn how you work.

Making time to do assigned homework

At the end of the phone screen, the interviewer may ask you to complete a programming task to return the next day no matter if you've done some live coding or just answered basic questions. It's likely this assignment will be a big question or a series of questions that will take you a few hours to complete.

The interviewer will tell you when and how you will receive the assignment, which application you should use to write your answers, when the homework is due, and how the assignment should be delivered.

And with this, the company just sent up a big, red flag.

The reason is not just because you're being asked to do a lot of unpaid work on your own time. Doing all that work is likely not worth your time if you're one of 100 candidates because the chances of your completed homework assignment leading to an interview is rather low.

On the other hand, being asked to do a homework assignment may signal that you're one of only a few candidates being considered. There's only one way to know for sure: Politely ask the interviewer about your concern after he tells you about the assignment.

For example, you can say, "My time is really valuable and I've got a lot of other jobs I'm working on. I don't mean to be rude, but can I ask you how many other applicants are in the running? I don't want to drop everything and spend time doing the assignment if there's not a good possibility that we'll be able to talk more about this open position."

If the interviewer responds to your liking, then you should ask him any outstanding questions about the assignment, especially if he's missed anything important such as when you'll receive the homework assignment in your email inbox.

When you hang up the phone or end your online call, drop everything, cancel the rest of your day's plans (even if it's just watching TV shows with your cat), decide when you'll eat dinner and take breaks, and block out a few hours to knock out your assignment.

TIP

If the assignment isn't due until late the next morning or early in the afternoon, set a time to stop working on it so you can get a good night's sleep. Wake up early enough the next morning so you have enough time to finish, review, and edit your code before you return your completed assignments.

TIP

If the interviewer says there are a lot of applicants or avoids answering the question, then you need to decide if you can beat the odds or if the homework assignment is a waste of your time. If you decide the latter, you can politely decline working on the assignment, say that you're removing yourself as a candidate, and thank the interviewer for his consideration. Then you can focus on other job opportunities, keep building your online reputation, and pay proper attention to your cat.

Avoiding disqualifying situations

As you experience the phone screen, at times you might feel like you're in a gladiator arena fending off attacks. You'll be asked questions that are designed to disqualify you, such as your salary expectations. They'll ask questions to see if it appears you're hiding something, cheating, or lying. What's more, how you answer questions during the phone screen can disqualify you. But we've got your armor and shield here so you know how to protect yourself.

Pausing exposes you

Don't keep pausing when you answer questions, such as saying, "Well, that's an . . . integer." That could tell the interviewer that you're looking on a site on your browser like Stack Overflow to get the answer to your questions. If you can't answer technical questions right away, that will tell the interviewer that you don't really know your stuff and you'll have some of your time released back to you.

Keep your shield up

You may have heard of the saying, "There's honesty and then there's transparency." The interviewer's primary job is to exclude candidates, and clearly showing your flaws will make that job easy for him. There are a number of other personal topics you can talk about to make his job easy:

>> Politics

>> Religion

>> Your background or heritage

>> How you think of others of different backgrounds

The interviewer may ask you two standard and infamous interview questions — what is your greatest strength and your greatest weakness? Think about those questions beforehand and be honest but not transparent.

For example, you can say a weakness is that you have trouble asking for help, which is honest. A transparent answer is that you're on medication to control a psychiatric condition.

Finally, as in an in-person interview, make sure you're always positive about former bosses and colleagues at companies you worked for.

When you test your answers to these and other questions during your mockup phone screen (like earthquakes in California, a mockup phone screen is a "when, not if" issue), ask for feedback from each of your friends if you think they would eliminate you or not. If they would, talk with them to form better answers that you can use during the actual phone screen.

Sidestep and parry salary questions

You may be asked about your previous salaries at your previous jobs, which is really a question about if you'll reveal proprietary information to another company and/or another person.

When you're asked this question, say something like, "I'd prefer not to reveal my previous salary right now because that's proprietary information."

If the interviewer asks you about what salary you want in the job you're applying for, don't answer the question directly. What the question really is asking is if you think of yourself more than the company.

Answer this question by saying something like, "I feel that I'd like to know more about the company and see how we like each other before we discuss salary. And salary's not the most important thing I'm looking for." After all, you also have to negotiate your salary as part of your overall compensation package, which you learn more about in Chapter 14.

How your friends react to these questions if and when you receive them during the mock phone screen may lead you to tweak your answers a bit, but you get the point: Be polite, be discreet, and don't show your cards until both you and the company come to the negotiating table.

3

Everyone's Testing Time

Level up your coding skills and learn from others how the company tests interviewees so you'll ace not only programming questions but the "soft skill" questions, too.

Absorb what you need to know about data structures and how to answer data structure questions the right way.

Learn about design patterns, including the singleton, factory, and façade, and then learn how to answer a recursion word problem.

Understand different sorting types, including bubble sort, merge sort, quick sort, and heap sort as well as the use cases for each.

Break down a puzzle problem, learn how to build your solution, and learn where to find puzzles so you can get better at solving them.

Chapter **8**

Testing Strategies for the Interviewee

The moment after you've finished your phone screen, or after you were asked to come in for an interview instead, you need to start preparing for said interview. Even if you don't get an interview after your phone screen, you need to start preparing as if you'll get that call for an interview any second.

In this chapter, we start by having you think like your interviewers to determine what questions you would ask a prospective employee — both technical questions and the infamous (if not dreaded) people or "soft skills" questions. This exercise will help you prepare for the questions the company may ask you.

If you feel you're weaker in one or more areas of the programming language(s) the company needs its new hire to know, then we tell you how you can level up your skills so that you can show them off when the interviewers ask you to write some code for them.

Finally, you learn how to canvass your network so that you can put together a proper mock interview, fix any issues, and be ready to slay the interview room. (Yes, metaphorically.)

Preparing for Questions the Company May Ask You

It may seem logical that you should find out what kind of questions the company will ask you before your interview so that you'll be prepared. Most people, though, ignore this opportunity because they're . . . optimistic that they can answer any question an interviewer asks. As a programmer, though, we suspect you're more thorough in everything from getting the code just right to getting your interview down cold.

Depending on how large the company is, you may be interviewed by the founders, a small number of people (like the entire programming team), or a cross-section of people from the team you'll be working with, folks from human resources (HR), and perhaps even executives such as a chief information officer (better known by the acronym CIO).

All these people will search online to find a list of questions to ask you about your programming skills. Your interviewers will also want to know about you as a person, so they will also ask the simple "soft skills" questions they've been asked in interviews before, such as where you want to be in five years, as well as look up similar questions to find out how you'll fit in the company's culture.

Searching online to find the top questions

To be adequately prepared, you should think like your interviewers and look up the potential questions on Google to find out what kinds of questions you may be asked. For example, if you're being interviewed for a Java programming position, it's easy to find websites that contain a list of Java questions as well as the answers.

Here are some common Java questions you'll find and you should know the answers to:

>> What are JDK, JRE, and JVM?

>> Why is Java not 100 percent object-oriented?

>> What are constructors in Java?

>> What is the JIT compiler in Java?

>> What is the final keyword in Java?

>> What is constructor chaining in Java?

>> What is polymorphism?

>> What are the different types of inheritance in Java?

>> What is a copy constructor in Java?

>> What is an interface in Java?

Don't just give back simple answers to the programming questions you receive, because your interviewers want to know that you understand the answers. That means your answers should be followed with an explanation of why the answer is correct.

Just reading the questions and understanding the answers aren't enough, though. Our brains are hard-wired to remember things if we write things down. So, get out your pen and paper and write down the questions as well as the answers you find from one or more websites. How you write them down so your brain remembers them is up to you, but the physical act of writing with pen (or pencil) on paper is how our brains work.

Don't believe us? Just Google "remember by writing down" (without the quotes) and see all the results that show why writing down is better than reading and even typing information. It may seem unnecessary, tedious, and even painful to you to write things down, but you can put your brain's improved performance to work in your mock interview as we discuss later in this chapter. We think you'll be amazed at the results.

Knowing how to answer soft skills questions

If you've participated in any job interviews, then you know about some of the standard "soft skills" questions interviewers ask to get a better idea of who you are as a person. You can get a soft skills question at any time from your interviewer or anyone on the interview panel — even a fellow programmer.

Just as with programming questions, you need to search online for the types of soft skills questions interviewers may ask you to be fully prepared. Here are some of the most common questions that are asked and how you should answer them.

Then, check out Chapter 16, where we discuss even more non-technical questions you may be asked and offer ideas to get you started thinking about how you could answer them during your interview.

Where do you see yourself in five years?

The correct answer is to talk about being a part of the company, growing professionally within the company, and actively contributing to the company's growth.

None of your answers to this question should ever be about you planning to leave the company, such as, "I want to get a better job somewhere else." If you say that, you'll be dismissed immediately and then you'll need take some time off to discover what it is you really want in life.

What are your greatest strength and greatest weakness?

The biggest problem with identifying your greatest strength is choosing the answer you want to use. If you can't figure out what your greatest strength is, think about the strengths you showed at work and/or school from your past experiences. Then think about which strength you think the company would benefit from the most.

The trap you can find yourself in when answering the question about your greatest weakness is trying to frame another strength as a weakness. For example, you might say, "My greatest weakness is that I'm a perfectionist. I like to do things perfectly." Being a perfectionist doesn't show the vulnerability required to be a weakness.

Instead, consider a similar response about perfectionism, but add some vulnerability. For example, "My greatest weakness is that I tend to be a little bit too obsessed with things, and sometimes I cannot complete a project, even though it's already good enough. I might spend too much time working on a small detail, polishing something that doesn't need to be polished."

TIP

When you give an example of a weakness that tells the interviewers it's something you need to work on, follow up by telling them how you've worked to turn that weakness into a strength. For example, you can say, "Over the years I've learned how to turn this weakness into a strength. What I've learned is that my attention to detail and my tendency toward perfectionism can be used in the right places to make sure that things are done properly. I've learned over time to know when things are good enough and I can move on. This has really helped me become a better developer."

How and why did you leave your last job?

Answer this question not by bad-mouthing the previous company, your bosses, and/or your coworkers. Always be positive about your previous company. Some reasons you can use for leaving your last job include:

> » I felt that my professional development had stalled, and I wanted to take some time off to grow my knowledge and contribute to the programming community by taking advantage of speaking and writing opportunities.

> » I needed to take time to get away from the computer screen for a little while and spend time with my family and some other important projects I needed to finish before I could return to programming.

> » I had some family issues that needed my attention, but I still managed to keep my feet in the programming waters by adding posts to my blog and answering questions on Stack Overflow.

These sample answers are honest, and talk about you and your situation at the time instead of denigrating others.

How do you deal with conflicts in your job?

This question is also one you want to answer without saying anything bad about anyone else. Your older family members were prepping you for an interview when you were young by saying, "If you can't say anything nice about someone, don't say anything at all."

Answer this question by saying that in some instances you realized you were wrong. Perhaps you said the wrong thing during a conversation, didn't say anything when you should have to resolve the situation, or didn't ask a question you should have asked. In this case, tell the interviewers how you learned from the situation by learning how to change your behavior: You learned to listen more clearly, think better on your feet, and talk with the other individual instead of withdrawing.

The interviewers aren't looking for you to show that you're perfect. If you did, the interviewers may think that you're being dishonest and/or hiding something. Instead, they want to know that you're a human being and that you're a better person now because of your past experiences.

TIP

Showing how you've grown personally over the years is even more critical if you're applying for a higher-level position such as a senior-level programmer or a manager of a team, where maturity at this stage of your life is an important asset.

Leveling Up Your Coding Skills

Your interviewers will expect you to write some code during your interview to show that you can actually solve programming problems. For example, you may receive an algorithm problem and be asked to put your solution up on a whiteboard in the room. This type of problem may not be something you've encountered much, if at all, in your previous programming jobs and/or in school, so you may need to brush up on these skills.

We're in a good time to be alive — we have the Internet, and so you can easily find websites that can help you level up your coding abilities and get you ready for these problems. What's more, you're reading this book, and we tell you about the types of questions interviewers like to give programmers.

This section covers Codility and LeetCode, two of the most popular testing and assessment websites available. These sites allow you to solve problems without the pressure of time and people looking at you. Your ego may be bruised when you find out you're not as good in some areas as you thought you were, but these two sites will let you take practice tests, get your confidence back, and avoid being embarrassed during the interview.

TIP

Codility and LeetCode provide services for companies to match a company's requirements with members and offer online assessments. So, don't be surprised if a company representative asks you during the phone screen or before the interview if you're a member of Codility or LeetCode. If you aren't, ask the company rep which website the company uses so you can create an account (it's free to join both sites) and begin taking tests and participating on those sites, as we discuss how to do later in this chapter.

Make an honest assessment

It's an axiom that the person we fear the most is the person in the mirror. Honest self-reflection is never fun, but it is liberating to have answers — or know where the answers are lacking. In the case of your upcoming coding test, ask yourself these simple questions:

>> Do you understand what all the data structures are?

>> Do you know what a queue is?

>> Do you know what a list is?

>> Do you know the difference between doubly-linked lists and an array?

>> Can you solve algorithm problems?

>> Do you understand the performance of various data structures and algorithms?

>> Do you know how to search in and sort algorithms?

>> Can you work with trees, lists, and various data structures?

>> Can you manipulate strings?

If you answered no or "kinda" to one or more of these questions, then it's time to feed your head (as the dormouse said).

REMEMBER

There's only a finite number of data structures. When you understand the handful of data structures and their related algorithms, you'll find that every problem you receive as part of your test will be related to those structures. So, as you take your practice tests, you'll see similarities, and by the time you finish your tests, you'll have an instinctive feel for how to solve any coding problem.

Getting up to speed with Codility

Codility is a product used by many companies to test candidates' skills, but the site also offers free resources and exams so programmers can get up to speed quickly.

Access Codility for Programmers at the website `https://app.codility.com/programmers`. Figure 8-1 shows the Codility for Programmers home page. Before you start, you need to sign up for a member account by clicking Sign Up in the upper-right corner of the webpage.

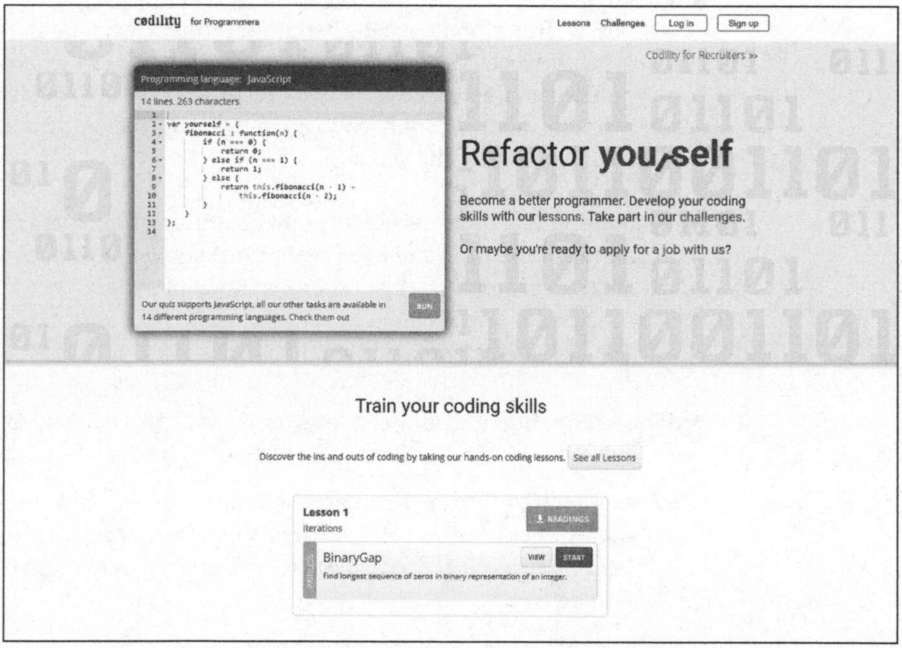

FIGURE 8-1:
After you sign up, you can log into your Codility account by clicking Log In in the upper-right corner of the screen.

Source: www.codility.com

The website allows you to read dozens of lesson documents in PDF format about topics including arrays, sorting, stacks, and algorithms. When you finish reading the lessons, you can take tests to check your knowledge. You'll receive results of your tests and you can take the tests over and over again until you get a perfect score on that test.

After you create your account, Codility sends you regular email newsletters. These newsletters offer news as well as "challenges" that allow you to solve a particular coding problem along with other Codility users who take up the challenge. (Codility says it has over 20,000 members.)

TIP

Challenges have time limits, so they're good practice for your interview because interviewers will ask you to finish a problem in a specific period of time. To take a challenge, log into the Codility website and block out an uninterrupted period of time (such as two hours) to finish it. If you submit what Codility calls a "golden solution," you'll have a Codility award on your profile that employers who use Codility can see. (You can also win prizes from challenges, but Codility reveals them only after you set up your account.)

Testing your skills with LeetCode

LeetCode is also a popular site for programmers who want to get up to speed. When you open the LeetCode website at `https://leetcode.com`, you have to sign up for an account by clicking on the Create Account button shown in Figure 8-2. After you create an account, you can sign in by clicking the Sign In link in the upper-right corner of the screen.

Like Codility, LeetCode has plenty of programming topics you can learn about, and you can take tests over and over again until you get a perfect score. You can also participate in contests against other LeetCode members.

LeetCode also has several additional features:

>> LeetCode offers lessons and tests from a variety of different large companies, including Amazon, Facebook, and Google.

>> When you participate in contests, you can win "LeetCoins." If you acquire enough LeetCoins, you can exchange them for trinkets such as a LeetCode T-shirt. When you get enough LeetCoins, you can redeem them for a Premium membership.

>> LeetCode has a variety of online forums so you can chat with other programmers online and build your online network.

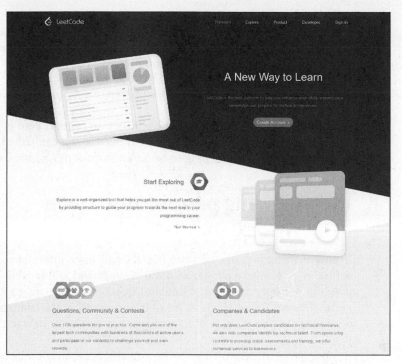

Source: https://leetcode.com

FIGURE 8-2:
The Create an Account button appears in the top section under the "A New Way to Learn" headline on the main LeetCode landing page.

>> You can purchase a Premium membership that includes access to LeetCode's best articles, online mock interviews, and more. As of this writing, a Premium membership costs $35 per month or $159 per year.

Canvassing Your Network

In previous chapters, we talk about imposing yourself on your friends to help review your cover letter and résumé, and help you with mock interviews. Your friends aren't the only people in your network, and it's likely they won't all be available to help when you need them, either. Is it time for dramatic music?

Cue the adventurous music instead because the situation is far from bleak for you, programming superhero. If you've read previous chapters, you know that LinkedIn is a premier resource for finding people who currently work at the company you are interested in or have worked at that company before. And if you're going to work for a large company such as Microsoft or Amazon, you'll also find books specifically written about the interview processes at those companies.

When the company calls to set up your interview, learn from the company representative how many people will be interviewing you and the interviewers' roles if you can. That knowledge will help you prepare your mock interview the right way. If the company rep won't tell you, then prepare as if you'll be meeting with an entire panel of interviewers — at least seven.

In the following sections, we outline how best to canvass your network so that you can learn more about the interviewing tactics of the company you want to work for as well as find folks willing to be a part of your mock interview team.

Interviewing people who have interviewed before

If you're fortunate, one of your friends will have interviewed at the company before — or knows a person who did. Your friend will be able to give you some pointers not only about what kinds of questions you may get but also what the entire process is like. If one or more friends work at the company, they may also be able to tell you about your interviewers so you know how to deal with them.

If talking to a friend isn't an option, you still have three paths to explore.

LinkedIn

If you have one or more LinkedIn connections who work in the human resources industry, contact them and ask if they know anyone who has worked at the company before. You'll obviously have much better luck if you're applying at a large company with many locations because such a person will be easier to find. What's more, the company likely has a fairly standardized interview process, so if your HR contact recommends someone at another location, the process at that location is likely the same as the one for the office in your area.

You can also search for the company directly in LinkedIn. A company search will also bring up the profiles of people who currently work for or who have worked at that company. If you're lucky, one or more of those people will be linked to one of your connections so you can ask your connection for a referral. Otherwise, you'll have to pay for and use InMail to make a connection and hope that person is happy to help you.

Programming forums

There are plenty of programming forums and groups on other social media websites such as Facebook and Reddit where you may be able to find people who work (or have worked) at the company. And don't forget to canvass programmer-centric websites, including Stack Overflow (https://stackoverflow.com; shown in Figure 8-3) and LeetCode, that have online forums; on those sites you can chat with other programmers and find out if they know anyone who works for the company you're interested in. Web-based programming forums and groups are less targeted than LinkedIn, but it's still a path with breadcrumbs.

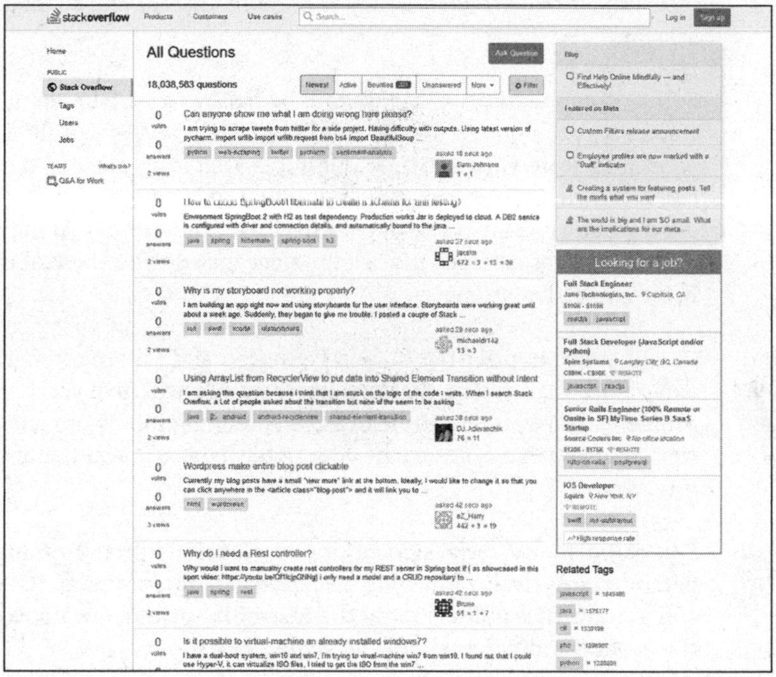

FIGURE 8-3: You have to sign up for or log into your Stack Overflow account if you want to ask a question.

Source: https://stackoverflow.com

In-person events

If you've applied to a job at a specific company in your area, then you should check out in-person programming events in your area. Your local newspaper and/or business journal as well as online meeting sites like Meetup (www.meetup.com) should have information about when the next event is.

Even in-person events aren't as effective as LinkedIn at finding people because you have no idea who will be at the event, let alone how many people will be there. But, like programming forums, live meetings are another opportunity to find the person you're looking for, or a person who can get you in touch with The One (or several Ones).

Finding people who will give you mock interviews

Chatting with others online and reading books (even this one) only take you so far. If your friends and other connections are in the same area you are, then you can get them together at a location that's convenient for everyone, such as shared office space that offers its conference room for rent and conduct a mock interview session.

Some, if not all, of your friends will be happy to participate in a mock interview. However, you don't want the mock interview to be friendly and easygoing. You want it to be nervous and intimidating — that is, as close to the real thing as possible. Only a realistic mock interview will give you the feedback you need to feel good when you start your actual interview. Therefore, you may not want to have all your friends as mock interviewers because during the real interview, you'll be in a room full of strangers.

TIP

One of your top priorities should be to find and talk to a programmer with more experience than you so that that programmer will give you harder programming problems and won't be afraid to ask challenging follow-up questions. More experienced programmers, such as your potential boss, await your arrival for the real interview.

REMEMBER

You can also use social networking sites, online programming forums, and in-person events to also find more experienced programmers. It's easy to find a person's experience online, but in the case of in-person events, you may have to ask the event coordinator whom you should talk to.

Schedule your mock interview

Your ability to schedule a mock interview will depend on how much time you have between the time you get the call from the company and when your company will be holding interviews. Many companies hold interviews during a block of time, such as during one week, so everyone in the company can get his or her other projects done and then concentrate on hiring the new employee.

When you talk to friends, strangers online, or strangers in person, ask them if they would be interested in participating in a mock interview at a convenient location like a rented conference room. Also be up front about your time constraints, and hopefully many of the people you talk to can accommodate your schedule.

You should block off at least four hours (that is, an entire afternoon) for the interview because you'll not only go through the mock interview but also receive feedback from your interviewers as well as people you may want to serve as observers (which we talk about later in this chapter).

Reward your interviewers well

You should approach all mock interview members either in person or online to ask them about what they want in return for their time and effort. People will want to be compensated in some way, and you'll need to figure out what that is — it could be a hearty meal, a gift card, or just a trade that you'll participate as an interviewer in the other person's mock interview.

You may need to give different gifts to different people. One way to do that is to give people a choice of what type of gift they want from a list of gifts you're willing to give. Your potential interviewer may have a suggestion for a gift instead, and you'll have to decide for yourself if you want to do that (or your budget may decide for you).

TIP

Don't serve any snacks or even meals until after the interview. During the interview, just serve water as that's likely all that's going to be served by the company during your real interview.

Prepare your interviewers

A mock interview is a good opportunity for your interviewers to role-play and give you a good idea of how to work with the personalities of your interviewers.

At least a day before you meet for the mock interview, think about who your interviewers are going to be, fire up Microsoft Word or your favorite word processing application, and type a one-page description for each person about what department each works for and what type of personality each is. For example, one interviewer can be very dominant, another can be nice, and another can be submissive.

WARNING

Don't type suggested questions into these descriptions. The mock interviewer is responsible for coming up with a list of questions based on the description. You're not supposed to know the questions ahead of time, just as with a real interview.

When you're done, print out each description and give it to each person at least a few days before the mock interview starts so that you know each interviewer knows his or her role. The interviewers will have some time to absorb it, form their questions, and rehearse their behaviors in their heads before the mock interview begins.

Here's a sample mock interviewer description that you can use as a starting point in building your own:

> You are an expert in Java, but you feel like your skills aren't being used at the company to their fullest extent. For that reason, you feel like any new person interviewing for a job better be at least up to your level or you don't even want to deal with them. You are dismissive of anyone who claims to know Java and doesn't have the skills to back it up and assume that everyone fits that category — unless interviewees prove otherwise.
>
> You don't really want to hire anyone because you feel threatened by anyone who could challenge your skills, so you'll be looking for flaws in even the highest qualified applicants. You also like to see how people react under pressure, so you often try to get a rise out of candidates by directly challenging them and being combative.

Include observers

The mock interview should also include at least two observers who will take notes about how you and your mock interviewers perform. These observers should sit out of easy sight, such as in the corner of the conference room. Feedback from people who aren't participating directly is invaluable to getting information that can help you during the real interview.

All this good feedback will also be invaluable for everyone else on the team since they may find themselves looking for another job someday. That argument may convince one or more people who are on the fence to join your mock interviewing team because they'll know they'll benefit from the experience.

Take notes to improve your answers

A mock interview is the perfect opportunity for you to take notes as you're asked questions and after you finish the coding test so you can understand what you're doing well and where you're falling short.

You should also write some notes right after the mock interview to get your impressions of the experience and any other thoughts about where you could do better. Your observers will be able to fill in some gaps in that knowledge as well, so be sure to get copies of their notes. (And don't be surprised if others in your mock interview group want copies of your notes to refer to the next time they have an interview.)

WHEN TO CONSIDER A SECOND MOCK INTERVIEW

Do you have to do a second mock interview? That depends on the feedback from everyone who participated in the first one. If you and many of the participants feel that they could do their jobs better, consider having a second interview after the first one if you and your mock interviewing team have the time that day. You may want to hold a second interview after people can have a break to eat, run errands, and/or decompress. Of course, you and your interviewing team can schedule the second mock interview on a different day if it works for everyone.

If you have the time and your interview team is willing, you may want to have a second interview after decompressing for a couple of hours and then see how well you fix some or all of your issues. However, some problems may need to be fixed during the time between your mock and real interviews, such as filling holes in your programming knowledge.

Getting Feedback after the Interview

Despite all the work you put in during the mock and actual interviews, you still may not get the job. If you received a letter from the company that you didn't make the cut, you still may want to call them and ask for their feedback.

For example, you could ask an honest question that's a little bit blunt: "Thanks for interviewing me. I'm really trying to improve my interviewing skills, and I would appreciate it if you could give me any feedback on areas I can improve. Or maybe you could just give me one thing I could work on to improve my interviewing; that would be awesome."

The person on the other line may be impressed enough that she'll give you that one thing and perhaps more. Write down those things as you receive them, and start working on fixing those things immediately. The next job interview is coming sooner than you may think. And it may come from the same company that rejected you if it believes you'll be an improved candidate for a future programming job opening.

Chapter **9**

Working with Data Structures: Garbage In Means Garbage Out

Y ou've likely used data structures in your job and/or you studied them in your computer science courses in school. Questions about data structures in interviews are as common as data structures themselves. Interviewers will want to know if you understand which data structures are used in particular situations so they know you're an efficient programmer.

If you need a data structures refresher, then you've come to the right chapter. We start by explaining the basics of data structures from lists and arrays to hashes, stacks, and queues.

Once you've soaked in everything about data structures, you learn what interviewers will ask you about them so you can show that your knowledge about data structures is, well, structured.

Finally, you learn how to get more in-depth information if you're still not feeling confident that you can answer interviewers' data structures questions correctly. These tips not only include refreshing your memory with good college and general market textbooks about the topic, but also where to find online courses so you can learn about data structures at your own pace.

Learning the Basics of Data Structures

A *data structure* is a particular method for managing, storing, and retrieving data. Data structures are similar in most programming languages. Even if you'll need to learn (or brush up on) a different programming language for the job, you'll be working with arrays, linked lists, hashes, stacks, and queues no matter what programming language your prospective employer wants. So, what we talk about in this chapter applies regardless of the language you're using.

Managing arrays and linked lists

Lists and *arrays* are the basic building blocks of data structures, but new programmers are often confused by them. All you may remember about them is that you didn't understand or know much about lists, so you were drawn to arrays instead.

The good and bad of arrays

Arrays differ from lists in several important ways:

>> An array is typically created at compile time if you're using a compiled language.

>> An array is of a fixed size.

>> Elements in the array are in a specific order. That means you can easily find out where an element in the array is and access that element quickly.

So, what's the price? (There's one for everything, isn't there?) Because the array is of a fixed size and is in a contiguous segment of memory while the program is running, applying any changes you make to the structure of the array, such as inserting or deleting one or more indexes, is a slow process.

Contrasting arrays with linked lists

A *linked list* is similar to an array in that it's a set of objects, types, or data that's arranged in an orderly manner. A list is linked together by a *node,* which you can think of like a link in a chain. There are two different types of lists: a single-linked list and a double-linked list.

The single-linked list, as you can probably tell from its description, is the simpler of the two list types. A single-linked list has a head node, and this node contains an element and a pointer to the next node in the list. The result is that lists are dynamic; that is, you can add and delete nodes at any point in the list. After you add or remove nodes, the pointers in each node update automatically so all the nodes in your list remain in perfect order.

And here comes the price again: When you want to access an element within a node, the list has to go through each node sequentially until it comes to the node that contains your element. And that process takes more time than you may expect at first.

REMEMBER

A linked list can (but doesn't have to) occupy a contiguous space in memory. Your computer may place the list anywhere in memory. What's more, your list can be changed on the fly after you compile your program.

A double-linked list is a set of lists linked together. One node at the end of the first list has a link to the second list, and the first node at the beginning of the second list has a link back to the first list. As you remember, any linked list, single or double, holds more memory than an array because a longer list holds more elements.

When do you use an array or a linked list?

The most important thing to know is that an array's size is fixed, and it doesn't matter how many indexes are populated within that array. So, the memory is going to be used for the entire size of the array even though not all the indexes are filled. This means you want to use an array when you know three things:

>> The size the array needs to be

>> How many elements will exist in the array

>> How to access elements in that array quickly, which we talk about later in this chapter

When you don't know how many elements you're going to need to store ahead of time, and you may need to add more elements over time, then you need to use a linked list.

For example, if you're entering a stack of résumés and you want to do so in a sequential manner, and you need to add a new résumé when it comes into your office, then you can add each new résumé to your linked list without having to worry about size limits as you would if you used an array.

Wrangling hashes

A *hash* is a data structure with two parts: a key and its associated value. It is used to map data of any size onto a set of data of a fixed size. It's useful in computer science to create a hash table or hash map data structure that maps a key to some value. *Hashing* is the process of doing that mapping through the use of a hashing algorithm.

This can be hard to get your head around, but we have a good example: a dictionary. (We don't care if it's the printed or online variety.) A dictionary has a key, which is the word you're looking up. The associated value, the definition of the word, comes with that key.

Hash crash

Here's the catch about creating a hashing algorithm: A key doesn't have to be associated with only one value. You can create two different hashing algorithms that have different values but have the same key. That leads to what is politely called a *collision,* and then you can't find the values you're looking for when you access the hash key without performing a secondary check of each hash key and see which one has the value you're looking for.

So, it's important to understand that you should make a hashing algorithm as unique as possible. If you access a hashing algorithm to find the associated value with it, such as a résumé you're looking for, you'll be able to find that data much more quickly than you would with a linked list or even an array because you're just accessing the hash key. That is, you don't have to wait for the list to go sequentially through each item in the list to find what you need or specify the index of an array.

REMEMBER

If an interviewer ever asks you what fields hashing is used in, remember to tell them it's used widely in encryption to determine the uniqueness of a file. Creators of popular hashing algorithms in the encryption world virtually guarantee that their hashing algorithm has a key with a unique data value — the file. It also means if you find that two files have the same hash, you can be virtually certain that the files are the same. (If that's not good enough, you can still double-check each file. We won't judge you.)

Create a hash map

Programmers keep track of how each hash key connects to its associated value (like a file) using a *hash map,* also called a *hash table.* Accessing a hash map to find associated values allows your application to get the element(s) it's looking for quickly.

When you create a hash map, you should create it so you have more keys in it than elements. That way, you can easily add more elements by simply assigning the element to a hash key that isn't being used.

TIP

A good rule of thumb when you want to avoid running out of space in your hash map is to double the size of the number of keys you need in your hash map and then round the number of keys up to the next prime number. For example, if you have 12 keys connected to elements, double the number of keys to 24 and then round up to the next prime number, which is 29. Having 29 keys will give you plenty of space to add elements to new hash keys when you need to.

Hashes are common enough in programming languages including Java, C++, and C# that if you're interviewing for a job that uses those languages, then you need to be prepared to show how to use a hash — especially a hash map — to store elements efficiently.

Learning about stacks in your kitchen

A *stack* is a straightforward data structure that holds elements. The order in which elements are removed from the data structure is known by its acronym LIFO: Last In, First Out.

The easiest way to visualize how stacks work is to look at the stack of dinner plates in your kitchen. Before you wash your dirty dishes and put them away, there's one plate that's currently at the top of the stack of plates in the cupboard. After you wash your dishes, you place the clean dishes on top of the stack, and the plate that was at the top of the stack is now somewhere in the middle. One of the washed (and dried) plates you added to the stack is now at the top. The next time you need a dinner plate, you grab the one at the top of the stack. That plate was last in, and first out.

When you have a stack of elements, you can write code to get the first element in that stack and do something with it. For example, if you want to spell a word in reverse, you can put all the letters of the word onto the stack starting with the first letter and ending with the last letter. When you take the letters off the stack and display them on the screen, you see the word is spelled in reverse.

You can tell that a stack is a simple and straightforward data structure to implement, so you can expect that an interviewer will ask you how to implement a stack in an application.

Learning about queues

You need to know about stacks so that you understand what queues are. The only difference between a queue and a stack is that you get elements from the queue using FIFO: First In, First Out.

A *queue* is a synonym for a line, so a queue data structure behaves just like a line to get into a concert to see and hear today's hottest singer: The first person in line gets in first, and the last person in line passes through the metal detectors and the double doors last.

Queues are useful when you want to process elements in the order in which they were received. For example, when you're creating a message processing application, you want to process the messages as they come in. When a message comes in, the queue would start up and enqueue that message. *Enqueue* means the program adds the element (the message) to the queue.

When the message is at the front of the queue and ready to be processed by your handy application, you *dequeue* the message. That is, you take it from the queue so your application can use it to do something, such as display the message summary on the screen.

TIP

If an interviewer asks you about how to use a stack, you can expect to receive a follow-up question about how to use a queue. That question may be about the properties of a queue, how a queue works, and how to implement a queue. In other words, everything we just told you.

Showing You Know Data Structures

So far, we've given you an idea of what interviewers may ask you about data structures. You need to be prepared to answer these questions and to do so the right way, and that's what this section prepares you to do.

TIP

If interviewers don't ask you about using data structures specifically, they may ask you about problems that require data structures to solve. Don't be shy in talking about the correct data structures you would use to solve the problem. Showing that you have high levels of competence and confidence when it comes to using data structures will further persuade your interviewers that you're the right person for the job.

Questions companies have asked interviewees

During a phone screen, the interviewer may ask you about using data structures and how you implement them. If not, it's likely interviewers will ask about using data structures during the actual interview to find out if you know which data structures to use in a particular situation.

Prepare for specific questions

Here's a list of basic data structure questions interviewers will likely ask:

>> What are the differences between a linked list and an array?

>> What is a hash and when would you use a hash and a hash map?

>> What is the difference between a stack and a queue?

>> When would you use a stack?

>> When would you use a queue?

>> How do you implement a linked list, a stack, or a queue?

One or more interviewers may also ask you about more complex data structures such as what a binary tree is, so if you feel you need to brush up on those sophisticated data structures, you learn how to find resources about them later in this chapter.

Know how to apply data structures

Your interviewers may ask you to write one or more algorithms on a whiteboard in response to questions that ask you to apply data structures. For example, they may ask you to:

>> Write an algorithm to traverse a linked list.

>> Create a linked list and then insert and remove elements from it.

>> Rearrange an array.

>> Reverse the order of a linked list or array — or both. If you write an algorithm for both data structures, you need to explain the differences in those algorithms.

>> Queue up messages to process them one at a time or process the most urgent messages first.

Typically, the questions that ask you to create algorithms are in the form of a word problem, such as reversing a string, to make you deduce which data structure is the one that will solve the problem.

Answering data structure questions the right way with Big O

As you write your algorithm, talk about what you're doing and why the data structure you're using is the correct one to get the result the interviewer wants.

Big O notation is the first concept to have in mind if you want to answer data structure questions correctly. If Big O reminds you of the tire company instead of a programming term, then what you need to know about Big O notation is that it's a method for measuring how much time it takes and how much space is required to execute an algorithm.

For example, an interviewer may ask what the Big O notation is for traversing a linked list to find an item within that list. Answering this question correctly requires you to understand that this is a linear search, also known as a sequential search, because you have to progress from one element to the next in the list until you find the element you're looking for.

TIP

If the interviewer asks how accessing a linked list differs from an array, the correct answer is that you can use Big O notation to access the exact index and get the element instantly, such as the element in O(4) to get the element within index 4.

As you talk about the data structure you're using in your algorithm, you need to cover the following talking points:

>> What a data structure is and does.

>> What the common operations on the specific data structure are.

>> Why you're using use data structure over another.

>> The speed of different operations in different types of data structures.

>> The data structure's set of operations that you can perform. For example, in a linked list you can insert and delete elements as well as remove a node from the list. You can also traverse the linked list to determine its length.

REMEMBER

If you want to score bonus points with your interview team, tell them about instances in the past when you've used data structures at other companies to complete projects. One example is how you used a stack in a particular situation. Showing your interviewers real-world examples is how you put smiles on their faces.

Finding More Detailed Information

If you have a programmer on your mock interview team who is more experienced than you are — or at least has interviewed with the company you're going to interview with — then you're already ahead of your competition.

When you prepare your mock interview, which we talk about in Chapter 8, you should encourage each programmer on your mock interview panel to challenge you, though they probably won't need any persuasion. They may give you questions that you can't answer right away and you'll need to find information online or even crack open another book to help you answer those questions and give you an even better understanding of data structures.

So, where do you start? We'd be remiss if we didn't suggest *Programming Interviews Exposed: Coding Your Way Through the Interview*, Fourth Edition by John Mongan, Noah Kindler, and Eric Giguere (Wrox). This book has in-depth examples about the data structures we discuss in this chapter and advanced structures including trees and graphs.

If you're not allergic to opening books and reading text on real paper (and likely you aren't, if you're reading this one), you should also check out computer science books at your local library or that you can purchase from Amazon or your local bookstore. You may already have used some computer science books in college courses but don't have them anymore, and this is a good opportunity to correct that error and have copies of these books near your desk for easy reference.

Books take up too much space, you say? Paper books are bad for the environment? Books aren't interactive?

Fair enough. Go online and use websites including LeetCode, which we talk about in Chapter 8, and Interview Cake (www.interviewcake.com) to hone your programming skills interactively.

Do you learn better by watching before doing? There are plenty of computer science courses available (for a fee) on a variety of different websites, including LinkedIn, Udemy, Coursera, Khan Academy, and more.

TIP

If you'd rather not pay for online computer science courses, there is a bounty of free online courses available from top-tier universities, including Harvard, Stanford, and MIT. The Computer Science Online website (www.computerscienceonline.org) contains links to these universities' online course websites where you can search for specific topics such as data structures and view a list of courses that match your search terms.

When you add up what you've learned in this chapter, where all these other resources are, and mock interviewers eager to lay down the gauntlet, the real interview will be a piece of cake, or easy as pie, or . . . we see you're drooling on the book, so go enjoy a tasty snack. You've earned it.

Chapter **10**

Identifying Design Patterns and Using Recursion

The overall goal of this book is to put you ahead of your competition to get the job you want. You may not succeed in your first attempt to get a job, but the fact that you have this book means you're dedicated to that goal, too. One of the most important aspects of a job interview that will set you apart is your ability to recognize and understand design patterns.

When can you expect to receive a question about design patterns? You'll most likely get these sorts of questions if you're programming in high-level C++, but you may also get design pattern questions if the job requires you to program in other object-oriented languages, including Java, Python, and Ruby.

This chapter starts by showing you how to recognize some of the common design patterns, including the singleton, adapter, and several other patterns. Next, you learn how to use recursion, which is a function present in many design patterns, to solve problems.

Then you learn what kind of recursion tests you may encounter in an interview and how to solve those tests successfully. Finally, we tell you where to find more recursion examples and resources online so you can hone your skills and dazzle your interviewers with your recursion prowess.

Recognizing Design Patterns

Don't feel bad if wrapping your head around design patterns only ends up giving you a headache. They are hard to understand in part because there are a lot of patterns to remember: 23 of them, to be exact.

Thankfully, some design patterns are more important than others, and it's these design patterns you need to know. This section not only tells you why you should use design patterns, but also about the essential design patterns programmers use.

WARNING

Many modern programming languages have eliminated the need for many of the 23 design patterns that exist, so you should check on the web and/or in a book about design patterns to find out if you will need to learn any design patterns beyond the ones discussed in this book.

Understanding the basics

In programming, *design patterns* are reusable solutions to common programming problems. They were modeled after design patterns in architecture — you know, the field where you build actual buildings, not the software term. A good example is an arch, which is a common architectural pattern used to distribute a large amount of weight across a span. You don't have to explain every detail of an arch to architects — they understand what an arch is as soon as you say the word.

The same is true when programmers tell you they're using a singleton in an application. You should know that a singleton means a single instance of an object. (Okay, it's only slightly more complicated than that, and we go into more detail about it later in this chapter.)

TIP

If you want or feel you need more information about all 23 design patterns for the job you're interviewing for, pick up a copy of the seminal book, *Design Patterns: Elements of Reusable Object-Oriented Software* by Gamma, Helm, Johnson, and Vlissides. You may hear this book referred to as the "Gang of Four" book in programming circles. This book was published by Addison-Wesley in 1994 and is the first book published about design patterns.

Knowing when to use design patterns

It's important to know design patterns, but they're not a be-all, end-all solution to every programming problem you have. It's tempting to simply add a design pattern because you think it's going to work only to find that the solution

>> is more complex than you thought it would be,

>> puts in a lot more lines of code than another solution, and/or

>> causes the program not to run at all after you compile it.

So, why do we have a chapter about design patterns in the first place? Because they're building blocks. Just as we used our fingers to count and add numbers when we were young, using fingers doesn't work when you're adding large numbers or multiplying numbers. When you add large numbers, you may add some numbers on your fingers when the situation calls for it.

The same is true when you're programming — design patterns are primary tools you learn in programming that you can use when they can perform the function you need.

TIP

When an interviewer asks you to solve a problem on a whiteboard, as you write the code you may find a design pattern that works — or you start to write the pattern and it doesn't work. In either case, tell the interviewers about the design pattern you're using, and why it's working or not working. If it doesn't work, discuss what you'll try instead. You may not solve the problem, but if you show that you know about design patterns and if and when to apply them, it shows you can think. Interviewers like that.

Learning about singleton, adapter, façade, and more

When you're asked about design patterns, you may only be asked if you know some of the common design patterns, what they do, and if you can provide examples of some of them and how they work. Let's prepare: place the bar down on top of your lap, keep your hands inside the car, and let's take a tour of seven common design patterns.

REMEMBER

Modern languages implement many design patterns right into their frameworks. So, after you read this section, you can check your programming language framework for design patterns.

singleton

We're starting with the most basic design pattern there is: the singleton, which is a pattern where there is only one instance of, and a global point of access to, an object or class.

For example, you can write a program that connects to a physical printer so that a user can print data from the program. Any time you need to print something, you don't need to use multiple instances of that printer because there's only one that's connected to the computer and has jobs queued up. So, a singleton design pattern works in this case.

factory

The factory design pattern allows you to create subclasses so that each subclass decides what objects it will create. Think of the factory design pattern as a smart creator that standardizes the way objects are created. Then you can create algorithms that can get specific objects because you know the factory design pattern assigned the attributes you need to the objects you want.

builder

A builder design pattern consists of a class that can build another object. The most common example is a string builder that you've probably encountered when you've created programs since most programming languages have string builders included in their frameworks. The string builder allows you to add characters to the string. When you're finished, you can construct the string.

adapter

An adapter design pattern matches the interfaces of different classes so both classes work together in your algorithm. Think of the adapter pattern as a home electrical plug adapter. Many older homes still have two-prong electrical plugs and nearly all modern electrical plugs have three-prong connectors. You can go to your local hardware store and buy a three-prong to two-prong adapter. When you plug the three-prong power cord into the adapter and then plug the adapter with the attached cord into the two-prong electrical plug, your electrical device turns on.

façade

One definition of a façade in the dictionary is a deceptive outward appearance. In the case of a façade design pattern, the pattern is not trying to deceive you; instead, it's a class that makes it easy for you (and/or the program user) to interface with a subsystem that's far more complex.

An example is the controls in a modern car — the steering wheel, gas pedal, and brake. All three are easy to interface with. Turn the wheel to turn the car in the direction you want to go. Press your foot on the gas pedal to accelerate. Press on the brake to slow down or stop. Easy-peasy.

You don't have to control or even know about the carburetor, the engine, the fuel injection system, or even the gear shifter in your car. You just drive the car using that simple interface that acts as a façade for the complex system that gets you where you want to go.

proxy

A proxy design pattern is just as the name says: an object representing another object. This pattern is often used as a security measure to protect a component or other object in your algorithm. For example, you can write a proxy class so only user account objects that contain the admin username can access the protected object.

iterator

The iterator design pattern sequentially accesses elements within a collection. When you know there is a data structure within a collection but you don't know what it is, the iterator pattern returns all the elements within the collection. Then you can see the elements within the collection in the order the collection stores those elements.

Knowing What You Need about Recursion

Now that you know the basic design patterns, it's time to learn about a nifty feature present many of them: *recursion*. Recursion is a feature that allows the algorithm to continue to call itself to solve your problem by breaking it down into smaller and smaller problems. (That kind of sounds like the process to find a new programming job, doesn't it?)

There are two different types of recursion: direct and indirect.

Direct versus indirect

Direct recursion occurs when the recursion function directly calls itself from within itself. For example, you may want to sort a big list of items such as information about all the businesses in a large metropolitan area. Your goal with your algorithm is to keep breaking the list down until you get the types of businesses in your area that you want to contact about potential programming jobs.

One thing you can do is use recursion to break the list in half and then sort two lists. Then break each of those two lists in half and continue that pattern until you have then two small lists of items you want to sort. Now you can sort the two lists together and get the master list of businesses so you can sell yourself and your skills (like your ability to use recursion).

Indirect recursion occurs when Function A calls Function B, and then Function B refers back to Function A. For example, if Function A is responsible for maintaining the hierarchy of a folder, then that function can call Function B that processes the files within that folder. Those features will continue to call on each other until there are no other files to process . . . provided you've added code in your algorithm to end the indirect recursion cycle.

Here's simple example of direct recursion:

```python
def is_even_direct(n):
    if n == 0:
        return True
    else:
        return not is_even_direct(n - 1)

def is_odd_direct(n):
    if n == 0:
        return False
    else:
        return not is_odd_direct(n - 1)
```

And an example of indirect recursion:

```python
def is_even(n):
    if n == 0:
        return True
    else:
        return is_odd(n - 1)

def is_odd(n):
    if n == 0:
        return False
    else:
        return is_even(n - 1)
```

The real stack overflow

A common problem with recursive algorithms, or recursive functions within an algorithm, is that you need to remember to include an end condition within the algorithm. This is true of both direct and indirect recursion. Fortunately, modern programming languages include classes so you can end the recursion after a certain number of recursion calls.

If you don't add the appropriate class, the algorithm will continue to call on itself repeatedly until it sucks up all of your computer's memory and you receive the dreaded stack overflow message. (Stack overflow isn't just the name of an important website.)

REMEMBER

If you're not sure if your programming language supports recursion, and which design patterns support recursion, you have three ways to find out: Check your programming language documentation and/or frameworks, search on Google, and find a design patterns book for the specific programming language you're using and read the chapter on design patterns.

Understanding Your Recursion Test

If you get word from mock interviewers and/or programmers who interviewed with the company before that you'll be asked about recursion, you should presume that an interviewer will ask you to solve a recursion problem.

Common examples of recursion algorithms include:

» The Fibonacci series

» The Tower of Hanoi puzzle

» Searching algorithms

» Copying a string

» Permutations such as combinations in a string of digits

TIP

Even if you don't receive a question to solve a recursion problem specifically, a question an interviewer asks you may require recursion to solve properly. In that case, be prepared to point out the recursion when you use a design pattern in your algorithm that solves the interviewer's problem.

Solving a recursion word problem example

We'll use a common recursion algorithm as an example of how to solve a recursion word problem: the palindrome. If you remember, a palindrome is a word (or words) or a number that reads the same backward and forward. Palindromic words include civic, kayak, level, madam, and race car. The last year that had a palindromic number was 2002, and shorthand dates such as 9/19/19 are also palindromic (at least if you live in the United States).

So, how can you find out if a string is a palindrome? When you begin to write your algorithm, start by having the program check the first and last letters of the word to see if they're the same. If they're not, then the word isn't a palindrome.

The next part of the algorithm will then check the second letter and the second-from-last letter in the word to see if they're the same. If those letters are the same, the algorithm will check the third letter and third-from-last letter and so on until you run out of characters in the word.

The easiest and most effective way to do solve this problem is by using a recursive function within your algorithm. All you have to do is write a function that compares the first and last letters. If they are the same, then the function shortens the string by removing the first and last letter of the word and then compares the first and last letters of the shorter word.

The recursive function calls itself repeatedly to repeat these actions with the word until there was a string length of one or zero, and then the function would end. You could also have the algorithm send a message to the screen that the word is a palindrome or not.

Don't believe us? This problem is easy enough that you can try yourself in any programming language you're using. See if you can solve it.

Finding more examples and resources

Though we're language agnostic in this book, it's easy to find recursion examples in the language of your choice. All you have to do is go to Google and type **recursive program examples** followed by the name of your programming language. Then you can browse through the results and view the pages that include samples.

TIP

Your interviewer may also ask you to implement some functions recursively instead of solve a recursion problem that already exists. In that case, you should also explain to your interview team about how to implement them iteratively as well. (Free reminder: *Iterative* means a loop is executed repeatedly until a certain condition is met.) Showing that you know the difference between recursion and iteration is another way to keep your interviewers smiling.

Chapter **11**

Sorting with Sorting Algorithms

Programmers don't use sorting algorithms that often in their daily work, but one or more interviewers will likely ask you questions about sorting because they want to know two things: your range of skill as a programmer and your depth of understanding in computer science. This chapter helps prepare you to answer those questions.

We start by giving you the full tour of standard sorting algorithms, including bubble sort, merge sort, quick sort, and heap sort. Then you learn when you need to use each sorting type to solve programming problems.

Next, we show you a common example of sorting one deck and multiple decks of playing cards. Finally, if you want to dive deeper into sorting, we tell you where you can find a variety of online resources so you can not only get more detailed information, but also view more examples.

REMEMBER

If you're applying for a senior software development position, then questions about sorting are practically guaranteed. Even if you're not asked a sorting question during the interview, you should think about mentioning sorting when you're solving another problem or when you're asked another question about programming so you at least let your interviewers know you studied sorting . . . and that you're ready to hit any follow-up sorting question out of the park.

Absorbing Common Sorting Algorithms

Fortunately, it's not important to know every sorting algorithm, and interviewers won't expect you to know them. What interviewers will expect you to know when you talk about sorting includes:

>> The most common sorting algorithms, and

>> The trade-offs between different sorting algorithms.

They will also expect you to be able to write down a simple sorting algorithm on the whiteboard in the interview room. So, as your docents in this chapter, we start your tour of sorting with a basic sorting algorithm: the bubble sort.

REMEMBER

For the sorting examples in this chapter, we'll use numbers because using them makes the concepts of sorting easier to understand. However, anything can be sorted with a sort algorithm. In most programming languages, all objects have some kind of value. Essentially any element can be compared to another element of the same type so the sorting algorithm will determine which is greater. For example, letters can be sorted alphabetically as they equate to an ASCII value, which is numeric.

Starting the tour with bubble sort

The bubble sort is perhaps the simplest . . . er, sort of sorting algorithm that you probably learned about it in your introductory computer science class in high school, community college, or university. A bubble sort is usually presented as a theoretical sorting algorithm. It isn't something you should use in code because it's very inefficient, as we soon explain.

The bubble sort algorithm traverses a list of numbers to sort and looks at the first and second numbers in the list. If the first number in the list is larger than the second number, the algorithm swaps the two numbers so the larger number is after the smaller one. If the second number is larger, or the first and second numbers are the same, the algorithm won't swap the two numbers.

Then the algorithm compares the second and third numbers in the list and swaps them if the second number is larger than the third. The sorting algorithm continues comparing subsequent pairs of numbers until it reaches the end of the list.

When you discuss a bubble sort algorithm in your interview, you should explain these three points:

>> The bubble sort algorithm is easy to implement.

>> The algorithm is stable because it only swaps numbers if one condition exists.

>> It doesn't take up a lot of memory.

You should also note that because the algorithm traverses the entire list, a longer list means the algorithm will take longer to complete.

There may be a need where a bubble sort algorithm may solve a problem, such as sorting a few post office ZIP codes, but if you have a longer list of ZIP codes to sort, there are faster and more efficient ways to sort ZIP codes (or any other numbers).

Expanding your knowledge about merge sort and quick sort

Merge sort and quick sort are the two go-to algorithms because they're more efficient than bubble sort. Both sorting algorithms are effective, easy to implement, recursive, and can be used to solve a wide variety of programming problems.

However, a quick sort algorithm can become too inefficient to use. In that case, you can supplement the quick sort algorithm with a merge sort or dump the quick sort code and replace it with a heap sort. Later in this chapter, we show you the different use cases for each type of sorting algorithm.

Divide and conquer with merge sort

Merge sort is a recursive algorithm that takes a list of numbers and splits the list in half. Then the algorithm continues to split each list in half until you're left with two numbers in several (or many) small lists.

Next, the algorithm sorts each small list so that the smaller number appears first in the list. The algorithm then merges one list with another list and sorts the numbers in the merged list correctly, and continues this pattern until the entire list output shows numbers sorted from smallest to largest.

The main advantage of the merge sort algorithm is that it's a much faster sorting method than bubble sort. In Big O notation, which you read about in Chapter 9, the average and worst-case compilation time for merge sort algorithms is $O(n \log n)$

where n is the number of elements you're sorting. In comparison, the running time for a bubble sort algorithm is $O(n^2)$.

A merge sort algorithm is also stable because it sorts all the numbers correctly. Also, the sort won't break if there are two identical numbers in the list; the algorithm will simply place the identical numbers next to each other in the sorted list.

The catch is that a merge sort algorithm uses more memory, and thus takes more time to process. That's something to consider if you have a large number of elements to sort.

Quick sort, the fastest of them all

The quick sort algorithm is also a divide-and-conquer recursive algorithm like merge sort, but like its name says, the quick sort wins the speed race against all other sorting algorithms.

The quick sort algorithm works by requiring you to pick one of the elements in a list as the pivot element, the element the algorithm will pick first. For example, if you have a list with ten numbers sorted randomly, the pivot element can be any one of the numbers in your list: the first element, last element, or any random element — it doesn't matter.

For example, suppose you have a list of 11 numbers, and you want to sort them with quick sort. Because you're an even-tempered kind of person, you pick the median element, which is the sixth out of the 11 numbers in the list, as your pivot element.

The algorithm splits the list in two: One list has all the numbers lower than the pivot number before the pivot, and the other list has all numbers greater than the pivot number. In sum, the pivot element is the only element in your list that is ensured to appear in the right place after the quick sort algorithm does its work.

Next, you'll write the algorithm to select a pivot number in each of the two lists. Those two lists will be ordered in the same way as in the first list. That is, the quick sort algorithm continues to split up each new list by moving all numbers before the pivot number before it and all numbers after the pivot number after it.

Eventually the lists are split to the point where there is only one number left in each list. Then the algorithm reconstructs the list by putting each number or set of numbers into the correct location in its parent list to the left or right of the parent list's pivot number.

For example, if the number in your final list is 5, and your parent list has a pivot number of 10, the quick sort algorithm will put the number 5 to the left of number 10 in the parent list so you have a bigger list. Now the algorithm puts this bigger list into its parent that has a pivot number of 20, so that parent will have three numbers in the correct order: 5, 10, 20.

The quick sort algorithm repeats this procedure until all the lists are put back together and then outputs the result — you see all 11 numbers in order with your original pivot number in the center.

WARNING

Quick sort has several drawbacks. Unlike merge sort, quick sort isn't as stable because the quick sort algorithm accesses memory space randomly. The result is that the algorithm may become confused and move elements that it put in the right place earlier in the sorting process into the wrong place later in the process.

The other issue is that if you have a large list of elements to sort, you not only run the risk of having a more unstable algorithm and thus an incorrect sort, but also the compilation time can increase from the average $O(n \log n)$ time to the worst-scenario of $O(n^2)$.

The more complex and powerful heap sort

When a list is too big for a quick sort algorithm to manage, programmers often turn to the heap sort, which is another common sorting algorithm. The heap sort finds the maximum element in the list and places it at the end.

For example, if your list consists of many numbers, the heap sort algorithm will find the largest number and put it at the end of the list. Then the heap sort will look at the remaining numbers and put the largest remaining number to the left of the largest number. The heap sort repeats this process until the algorithm sorts all the numbers correctly. Best of all, you'll get compilation time that matches the average of quick sort — $O(n \log n)$ — and heap sort doesn't use much disk space and memory on your computer.

Understanding use cases for each sorting type

We've talked about some of the use cases for implementing different types of sorting, but in real life, you'll likely use one or more sorting techniques to make your program run as efficiently as possible.

As we said earlier in the chapter, the bubble sort algorithm is primarily used as a teaching tool and may only be used with very limited lists. In your job, you're going to use the more common merge sort, quick sort, and heap sort algorithms by themselves or combined with another sorting algorithm.

A linked list

A linked list, which we discuss in Chapter 9, doesn't place its elements in a contiguous block of memory; a linked list stores its elements in random memory locations and uses pointers to connect each element in the list.

If you need to sort a linked list, merge sort is the best approach because the merge sort algorithm takes the entire list and splits it until the entire list is in the proper order. A quick sort algorithm has a difficult time finding elements in random memory locations so the compilation time will be quite slow.

You also can't use a heap sort to sort a linked list because a heap sort uses a tree-like structure, which is the antithesis of a linked list structure.

Memory restrictions

You may encounter memory restrictions when you try to sort your list. In this case, a merge sort works much better than a quick sort.

For example, elements in your list may be large files that won't fit into memory, but the merge sort algorithm can split up those files and sort them together so each individual file doesn't suck up all your memory. Each file is linked together so after the algorithm outputs the information in the first file, the computer will dump that file from memory and fill it with the second file so it can run.

Partial sorts

If you have a list that's partially or mostly sorted, then merge sort is fastest as the algorithm splits each list in two. So, because there isn't much to sort, the algorithm compiles much more quickly. If you use a quick sort algorithm, it will re-sort the list from scratch through the use of pivot elements, and it will take longer for the algorithm to return a result.

Solving Two Sorting Examples

So, now that you know about the common types of sorting algorithms you can use and when to use them, let's put your sorting prowess to the test. We'll use a test that combines two sorting algorithms together — quick sort and merge sort — into one program that sorts a deck of playing cards.

TIP

We suggest you grab a physical deck of playing cards so that you can visualize what we're doing in this upcoming section. Bookmark this page, put this book down, and go fish a deck out of your junk drawer or drive to your nearest store to buy one (or just order a deck on Amazon), and come back to this section after you have the deck next to you. Popular brands include Bicycle and Bee. Using a physical deck to illustrate what we're saying will help you remember sorting better than the Solitaire game on Windows or card games on the web.

Sorting one deck of cards

Before you start to sort your deck of cards, you'll need to assign a numerical value to each card so your sorting algorithm can keep track of all the cards. A standard deck contains 52 cards (excluding any jokers that come with the deck), so it's easy to number a newly opened deck. For example, you can use 1 to 13 for ace to king in the spades suit, 14 to 26 for the hearts suit, 27 to 39 for the clubs suit, and 40 to 52 for the diamonds suit.

Then you can add code to shuffle the cards. When the cards are listed in random order, you can use two sorting algorithms that will give you the results you want with the fastest compilation time. If you've been following along with us, you know what that means: using a quick sort and keeping a merge sort at the ready if quick sort fails.

TIP

If you don't know how to add code to shuffle cards, you can easily find this on Google by searching for "programming shuffle deck of cards" and you'll see a number of sites on the results page that show you how to do this in a variety of programming languages.

You'll start with a quick sort, so you'll need to pick a number in your list that represents a card you want to use as the pivot number. If you need to use a physical deck of cards, shuffle them and then pick one at random and tie it to the number in the list. For example, if you select the jack of spades, use the number 11 as your pivot number.

All cards numbered before the number 11 are in one list and all cards numbered after 11 are in the second list. Then you'll need to pick a new pivot number in each of the two lists. As the quick sort algorithm continues to divide the list into smaller lists depending on the pivot number in each list, you'll eventually sort the entire list.

What happens if your quick sort algorithm doesn't sort all your cards so that you see all the cards in their proper order? That's when you add a merge sort after the quick sort so you can split the quick sort algorithm's sorted list. The merge sort algorithm will complete a proper sort and output the list without taking up too much more of your time.

Sorting many decks of cards

Earlier in this chapter, we talked about a use case where you can use a merge sort algorithm to break up a large file because that one large file can't fit into your computer's memory. Another way to think of this use case is that you need to sort all the cards in ten decks, which is not such a far-fetched scenario if you find yourself working for a casino.

If you had ten decks of physical cards — and we're not suggesting you buy ten physical decks unless you get a really great deal — you can only pick up one deck of cards at a time because you only have two hands. And your computer can only work with so many cards because it has only so much memory.

So, you need to use your programming skills to make the computer do the sorting work, and the way you do that is by using a merge sort algorithm. This is a process that requires a numbered list to digest, so here we go:

1. Create an array for the cards in all the decks.

2. Assign numbers to all the cards in all the decks sequentially from the ace of spades in the first deck assigned numbers 1 to 52, the second deck assigned numbers 53 to 104, and so on until you reach the king of diamonds in the tenth and final deck that has the number 520.

3. Scramble the numbers in each deck.

4. Use the merge sort algorithm to break down the card numbers in the deck into smaller lists so your computer's memory can handle those lists.

5. Wait for the algorithm to finish reconstructing and sorting the master list of all the cards in all ten decks.

When you view the output, every card in each suit within each deck will appear in their proper order from ace to king. Slicker than a box of rocks.

Getting More Examples and Researching Resources

We've told you about common sorting features, shown you some sorting examples, and explained some use cases for different sorting algorithms. However, you may find this information nice but a bit lacking because you need sorting information specific to the programming language the company wants you to use.

What's more, there are more complex sorting algorithms out there, and the ones we've covered in this chapter are definitely lacking because you need to know more advanced sorting methods for your job interview.

We're here for you. Hop onto Google and search for "sorting algorithms" and you'll see a list of algorithms at the top of the screen that include visual diagrams of each one. Just click the sorting algorithm name or its associated diagram to refine your Google search and display websites that only discuss that algorithm.

Loads of reading material

There are some good websites out there that will give you more in-depth information. You can start with the Wikipedia website that contains charts and examples including the deck of cards example. Since Wikipedia is managed by the entire Internet community, it isn't as well-regarded as other sources of information, and in the case of Wikipedia's sorting algorithm article, there's a warning at the top of the page (as of this writing, anyway) that says there aren't enough links to reliable sources.

An excellent online resource is the GeeksforGeeks website (www.geeksforgeeks. org/sorting-algorithms) shown in Figure 11-1 that has in-depth resources about many sorting algorithms and examples of those algorithms in a variety of programming languages.

When you scroll down the page, you'll also find articles, frequently asked questions (and answers), a large number of coding problem examples and solutions, as well as links to practice sorting problems and quizzes.

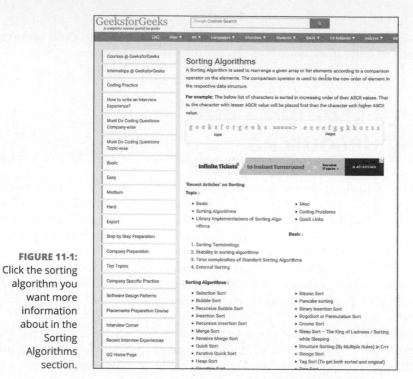

Source: www.geeksforgeeks.org

FIGURE 11-1:
Click the sorting algorithm you want more information about in the Sorting Algorithms section.

Moving examples

If you're more of a visual learner, more than a few websites contain animations of sorting algorithms so you can see how each one operates. Animated examples also illustrate the advantages and disadvantages of using each one. Just type (without the quotes) "sorting algorithms animation" into the Google Search box. The results page shows a list of sites as well as links to several animations on YouTube.

The site at the top of the search results is Toptal (`www.toptal.com/developers/sorting-algorithms`), shown in Figure 11-2. In the table at the top of the page, click one of the animations that shows how an algorithm sorts a list. For example, if you click the animation in the Random row and the Merge column, you'll see how the merge sort algorithm reorders the random items in the list to create a neatly ordered list.

Underneath the list you can change the conditions of the animation. For example, if you want to learn more about the quick sort algorithm, click Quick Sort to open a page that lets you view the animated examples for the quick sort algorithm and gives you more information about the algorithm and how it's used.

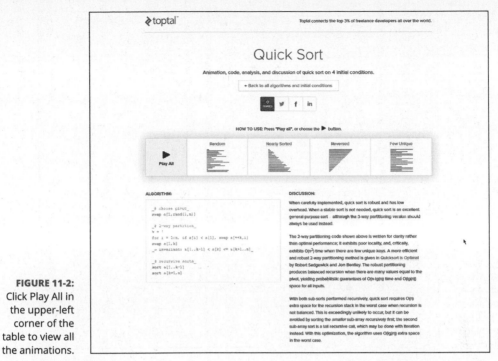

FIGURE 11-2: Click Play All in the upper-left corner of the table to view all the animations.

Source: www.toptal.com

Finally, when you scroll down to the bottom of any page on the site, you'll see links to job interview guides for various programming languages.

Visualize the sort, Luke

If the animations don't quite cut it and you prefer to see each step of the sorting process instead, check out the HackerEarth website visualizers at www.hackerearth.com/practice/algorithms/sorting/merge-sort/visualize. In Figure 11-3, you can see a sample for a simple merge sort.

Under the array of numbers you see in the center of the screen, you see the text 1/99, which means this is Step 1 in the process that has a total of 99 steps (and we confirmed there really are 99 steps in this visualization exercise).

Proceed to the next step by clicking the right arrow button to the right of the step number. As you go through each step, you see the result of each step in the Visualize section as well as a brief description of what's happening in the Steps section. As you keep clicking the right arrow button, you see the next step in the process. The step number appears to the left of the right arrow button, which in Figure 11-3 is Step 3. You can even change the array size and array values if you want.

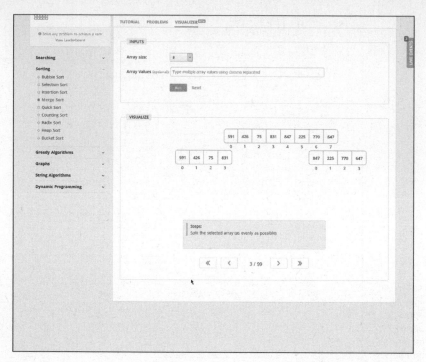

FIGURE 11-3:
The third step
on HackerEarth
shows the initial
array broken into
two separate lists.

What's more, if you prefer to visualize how other sorting algorithms work, click one of the sorting types in the sorting list at the left side of the web page — the list includes a number of sorting algorithms we haven't covered in this book so you can feed your ravenous brain.

Chapter **12**

Solving Puzzles Is Fun

During your interview, it's likely an interviewer will ask you to solve a programming puzzle. Not only is a puzzle is a good way to test your programming prowess, a puzzle also enables the interviewer (or group of interviewers) to see your problem-solving skills and how both sides of your brain — the logical and the emotional — respond as you work your way toward a solution.

We start this chapter by letting you in on what kind of puzzle problems an interviewer may ask you. Once you know that, we tell you the steps to solving a puzzle, including breaking down the problem and then building your solution.

Next, we talk about why an observation of your problem-solving skills is what interviewers want to see, what you need to focus on as you solve a puzzle, and the importance of talking with your interviewers as you work on your solution.

Finally, we show you where you can find other resources for solving puzzles, including books as well as websites that produce new puzzles you can solve on your own or in competition with others.

Knowing What Kind of Problems an Interviewer Will Ask

When one or more interviewers ask you to solve a puzzle on a whiteboard in the interview room (or even on a large notepad if a whiteboard won't arrive until Tuesday), most puzzle questions come in one of two forms. (Yes, we said *most* puzzle questions as there is a wide variety of puzzle questions an interviewer could ask.) One puzzle will be in the form of implementing a data structure, and the other will be in the form of implementing an algorithm that works on a particular data structure.

Good news, everyone: There is a finite number of puzzles that take on one of these forms.

TIP

If you're not sure whether the puzzle is going to come in one of the two forms we mention, start by finding puzzles that don't fall into these two forms. (You learn more about finding programming puzzles later in this chapter.) You should also ask your mock interviewing team to come up with two programming puzzles: one that fits one of these two forms and one that doesn't, so you can feel ready for any curveballs the real interviewers throw your way.

You should also be ready to answer logic or "brain teaser" puzzles that have nothing to do with computer science or programming. Instead, these puzzles are designed to learn how you solve problems. For example, one famous Microsoft interview question asks why manhole covers are round. Later in this chapter, we let you know how to prepare for brain teasers like this, too.

Solving a Programming Puzzle

You start to solve a puzzle by preparing your brain to understand it. If you don't, you may find yourself solving the wrong problem and find yourself intensely embarrassed and possibly dismissed from the interview room after you finish writing your wrong answer on the whiteboard.

So, here's what you need to do to be careful and understand the problem from the outset:

>> **Read the problem slowly three times.** If the problem isn't written down, write down the problem as the interviewer says it. Then repeat the problem orally to the interviewer and make any corrections. When you've confirmed the text of the problem, read it slowly three times.

>> **Engage in active listening.** For example, you could say something like, "When you said this, my understanding is that . . ." and then ending your sentence by asking if you're correct. If not, write down the interviewer's clarification.

>> **Ask any follow-up questions that come up after you read or hear the problem.**

WARNING

If your interviewers become agitated by you taking so long to understand the problem or start pressuring you to get started on and/or finish the problem quickly, you should remind them that you take the same approach with any problem you encounter in your job. This approach not only ensures that you get the solution right the first time, but it ends up saving time in the long run. If that argument doesn't convince your interviewers, perhaps it's time for you to thank them and leave since they've told you what the job and their company culture is like.

Breaking down a problem

Once you understand the problem, you need to break it down to its basic level that has a simple solution. For example, if an interviewer asks you to implement a sorting algorithm, you could use a simple solution as a starting point that you can keep in your head or write down as you start to build your final solution.

In this case, think about just three elements that need to be sorted. Can you solve that manually? If so, then go step by step and write down how you solved the problem.

TIP

A whiteboard will likely be on one of the walls in the interview room, and an interviewer will give you a marker and an eraser to work with. A notepad will suffice during practice if you don't have a whiteboard at home, but when you go through a mock interview, you should ensure that you find a location that has a whiteboard so you can accurately replicate the actual interview as much as possible. You'll feel the difference between writing on a notepad by yourself and writing on a whiteboard in front of several people.

Here's a more complex example:

The problem the interviewer wants you to solve is to reverse a string. How would you do that manually?

You could create two columns in your head or on a piece of paper with the left column containing the original string and the right column containing the reversed string. Then you would take the right-most letter in the original string and write it down as the first letter in the right column. Then you would take the right-most letter that remains in the left column and add it after the first letter in the right column. You would continue this process until the string is reversed.

Building your solution

Now that you've seen how to break down a problem, the next step is to apply that process to a more complicated version of the problem. Since you were able to sort three elements successfully, try sorting five elements, and then ten elements.

REMEMBER

By this time, you should be talking with the interviewers about what you've done to break down the problem and how you're going to build your solution. Your interviewers likely won't be able to see how you're putting the solution together on paper (and can't read your mind as far as you know), so it's important to tell them what you've done. If you haven't talked up to this point and don't intend to, you will anyway because the interviewers will ask you what you're doing and keep peppering you with questions as you work.

As you solve problems that are increasingly complex and gain confidence, the algorithm you're going to use for the interviewer's problem should become apparent. You can then take the steps needed to solve the actual problem.

For example, in the case of reversing a string, you would quickly find the algorithm to create that should look something like this:

1. **Determine the length of the string.**

2. **Use this to figure out the last letter in the string.**

3. **Copy the last letter of the string to the new string.**

4. **Reduce the length of the string by one and repeat until the length is 0.**

When you're confident that those steps will work for any input size, start writing *pseudocode*. The term *pseudo* means not genuine, and so this is not the genuine code you're going to use when you write the solution on the whiteboard. Instead, pseudocode is an informal, high-level code meant for human reading.

For example:

```
length = originalString.Length;
String newString = "";
While (length != 0) {
    newString.concat(originalString[length-1];
    length = length - 1;
}

Return newString;
```

After you write pseudocode for each step, translate that pseudocode into actual code the computer will understand. Write down input and see how the code processes it. If it works, then you're ready for the next step: looking for edge cases — that is, scenarios that will break the code you've written.

For example, what if the list of elements that you have to sort has no items or just one item in it? What happens if you get the opposite problem and you have a lot of items to sort? Or the data is invalid for some reason? The interviewers won't expect you to be able to solve all edge cases, but you have to tell them what the edge cases are and what will happen with your code if an edge case happens.

These are the steps you need to build your solution, but what happens if you fail to solve the problem?

Realizing What Interviewers Want

We have more good news: When you get a puzzle problem, your interviewers aren't looking for a solution. It would be nice if you provided one, but that's not what they're after.

REMEMBER

Interviewers want to know how you break down problems and work to create solutions. This explains why we're so insistent that you need to talk out loud as you write your solution so your interviewers can follow along. Your ability to take the complex and make it simple is how you'll show your interviewers that you're a good programmer worthy of being hired.

What's more, you don't have to worry about getting the syntax of your code perfectly correct when you write the solution on your whiteboard. This is another "nice to have" feature, but what your interviewers really want to know is if the problem-solving steps you take result in a correct algorithm.

Unlike programming problems, there isn't a way to really prepare for brain teasers or other logic puzzles even if you talk to someone who's interviewed with the company before. If you're lucky, the interviewer will ask you the same brain teaser question you knew about from talking with company employees, and you've had a chance to prepare for it.

However, if the interviewer is like a good math teacher who knows students share tests with friends — and the friends hope they get the same test so they can ace it — the interviewer will change the question from the previous interview. In this case you'll realize the answer you studied doesn't work and you'll have to think fast.

So, just keep things simple and remember that your job is to break down the brain teaser problem just as you would a programming problem, because that's what your interviewers want to see — how you work when you're presented with a problem.

Getting Better at Solving Puzzles

Take every opportunity to solve programming puzzles and even brain teaser puzzles that you find in books as well as online. Just like an athlete, you need to train your brain to think about breaking down problems. (You may want to train your body, too, since a healthier body leads to a healthier brain, but that's just a suggestion.)

Though there are an infinite number of possible problems an interviewer can ask, there are also only a finite set of algorithms that operate on data structures. So, once you know these algorithms, you'll have the toolset you need in your brain to solve any set of problems. Our brains are designed to instinctively recognize patterns as we work to solve problems, and the same is true in programming. As you work on more problems, you'll feel the rush that comes when you realize instinctively that a problem looks familiar to one you did earlier.

REMEMBER

Even if you have mad programming skills, you likely haven't had to solve algorithm problems in your current or past jobs. You still have to train your brain just like any other programmer to get your brain in the right frame of mind, though your skills may get you up to speed more swiftly than the average bear.

Working on puzzles in books

You can access websites that allow you to solve problems interactively. However, you may want to look at books that contain puzzles first. Working on puzzles in books and writing down the answers on paper (or in the book itself) has an advantage over working through problems online in that reading problems in books more accurately reflects the type of questions you'll receive during your interview.

REMEMBER

When you're in the interview, you're not going to have a computer in front of you. You'll either be seated at a table facing a panel of interviewers or sitting at the same table with one or very few interviewers depending on the type of company interviewing you. So, you'll be working out puzzles on paper or on a whiteboard instead of on a computer screen. By practicing puzzles in books beforehand, this situation will feel more comfortable than if you only worked out puzzles onscreen.

Where do you find a book with problems in it? Our first choice is the 2018 book, *Programming Interviews Exposed: Coding Your Way Through the Interview*, Fourth Edition, by Eric Giguere, John Mongan, and Noah Kindler (Wrox). This book contains three different chapters about solving different types of brain teasers, graphical and spatial puzzles, and knowledge-based questions.

If that isn't enough for you, the self-published book, *Cracking the Coding Interview*, Sixth Edition, by Gayle Laakmann McDowell contains 189 programming questions and solutions. Though this book is a bit older than *Programming Interviews Exposed* — as of this writing, McDowell's book was last published in 2015 — you'll find the practice problems are still valid and worth the time and effort to solve.

TIP

If you buy one or both of these books, you should set aside a block of time on a regular schedule and go through as many problems as possible through one or both books during your scheduled practice time. Though the books we've recommended include solutions to the problems, start by writing down the problem, closing the book, and then trying to solve the problem yourself.

Only after you've solved the problem (or you've become frustrated trying to solve the problem) should you open up the book and see how well your solution matched up with the one the author has or what step(s) you missed in solving the problems. Then, with that knowledge in mind, go on to the next problem and solve that. You'll be amazed at how quickly you'll solve practice problems after you've been working on them for a while. You may even start to find yourself looking forward to problem-solving time.

Searching online to hone your solving skills

Books only have a specific number of problems, but there are plenty of programming and logic puzzle websites online. Some of these sites may allow you to solve the problems interactively, but resist this temptation as interactive solutions won't duplicate the conditions in your interview.

You may want to search for puzzles for your specific language, such as typing **programming puzzles Java** in Google if you need Java-specific puzzles. However, as this is a language-agnostic book, we provide five valuable resources for programming puzzles and a bonus brain teaser website for your enjoyment.

CodeKata

CodeKata (http://codekata.com) is a blog that claims that "experience is the *only* teacher" (see Figure 12-1).

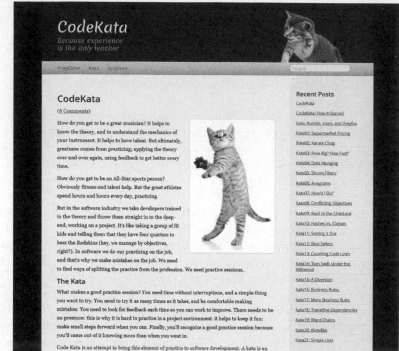

FIGURE 12-1:
The CodeKata website contains a list of programming exercises that encourage you to practice, practice, practice.

Kata is a karate exercise where you repeat a form many times (wax on, wax off), and blogger Dave Thomas has a large repository of exercises that Thomas says takes about 30 to 60 minutes to solve. Thomas freely admits each problem is unlikely to have a single correct answer.

When you click the title of a puzzle under "Recent Posts" on the CodeKata main page, you'll open a web page that tells you about the puzzle and the goal. You can also leave comments about the puzzle and for Thomas on the site.

Codility

In Chapter 8, we talk about Codility as a place where you can take online lessons about all sorts of programming topics to sharpen your skills. If you feel like you have a good grasp of the skills you need, then put them to the test by going to the Codility for Programmers website (https://app.codility.com/programmers) and then clicking Challenges in the upper-right corner of the website to accept the site's latest challenge or work on past challenges (see Figure 12-2).

Figure 12-2 screenshot:

codility for Programmers — Lessons Challenges [Log in] [Sign up]

UPCOMING CHALLENGES:
CURRENT CHALLENGES:

Niobium 2019 codility

PAST CHALLENGES:

Zirconium 2019 — asseco
Yttrium 2019 — zalando
Strontium 2019 — codility
Rubidium 2018
Arsenicum 2018 — codility
Krypton 2018 — okta
Bromium 2018 — betsson
Future Mobility
Grand Challenge — PETUUM
Digital Gold — ASML
Selenium 2018 — adyen
Germanium 2018 — zalando
Gallium 2018 — codility
Zinc 2018 — Grab
Cuprum 2018 — CHALLENGE
Cutting Complexity — ASML
Nickel 2018 — Avature
Cobaltum 2018

Niobium 2019

Start date: May 6, 2019. 5 p.m. UTC

[START CHALLENGE]

Invite your friends to this challenge!

[Tweet] [Share 4]

codility
The Niobium Challenge

Kicking off May is The Niobium Challenge, hosted by Codility.

Here at Codility, we help companies grow their dev teams by assessing their candidates' technical skills online. We're growing our team too - so if you're interested in helping us refactor tech recruiting, check out our open positions.

Good luck solving this Challenge!

[Check our opening]

Stats:

| 3456 started | 317 silver awards | 241 golden awards |

Hall of fame:

Vikram Panwar	Time: 9 minutes
Tadeusz Sznuk	Time: 13 minutes
Alex Rhatushnyak	Time: 22 minutes

FIGURE 12-2:
You can view a list of current or past challenges on the left side of the Codility for Programmers web page.

Source: www.codility.com

TIP

You'll need to sign up for a Codility account if you want to participate in a challenge. After you click the Start Challenge button in the upper-right corner of the home page, you'll open a web page that tells you how much time you'll need to set aside to finish the challenge and if there are any opportunities for you to pause while you try to solve it.

LeetCode

We also talk about LeetCode's many resources in Chapters 8 and 9, and this website (https://leetcode.com) also has numerous questions in a wide variety of categories that you can solve, as you see in Figure 12-3.

TIP

You view questions in all categories by default. Within the table of questions you see the question title in the Title column; click the title to open the question page. If there's a page icon in the Solution icon, that means the question page includes solutions to the question in various programming languages. If you want to try to solve a problem that doesn't have a solution, click a title that doesn't have a Solution icon to the right of the title name.

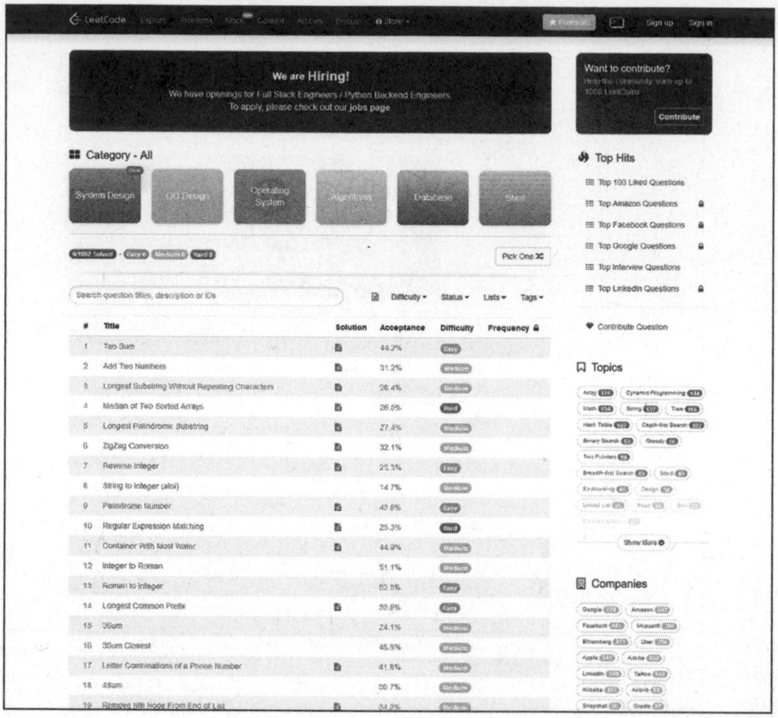

FIGURE 12-3: Click a category name at the top of the LeetCode web page to view questions within that category.

Source: `https://leetcode.com`

Programming Praxis

Programming Praxis (`https://programmingpraxis.com`) is a minimalist blog that regularly posts new puzzles for you to solve (see Figure 12-4).

The question appears on the page so you can work on the exercise at your leisure. Click the title of the exercise (such as the Van Eck Sequence shown in Figure 12-4) to open a page that not only contains the problem but also potential solutions in the comments. You don't even have to sign up for an account to leave your own solution or comment in the Comments section.

View past exercise categories by clicking the Exercises option in the red menu bar at the top of the web page and then clicking a selection in the menu. The list of exercises appears in its own web page with three links: one to view only the exercise, one to view a summary of the solution as well as user comments and/or solutions, and one that shows the solution code in Scheme, the site's preferred programming language.

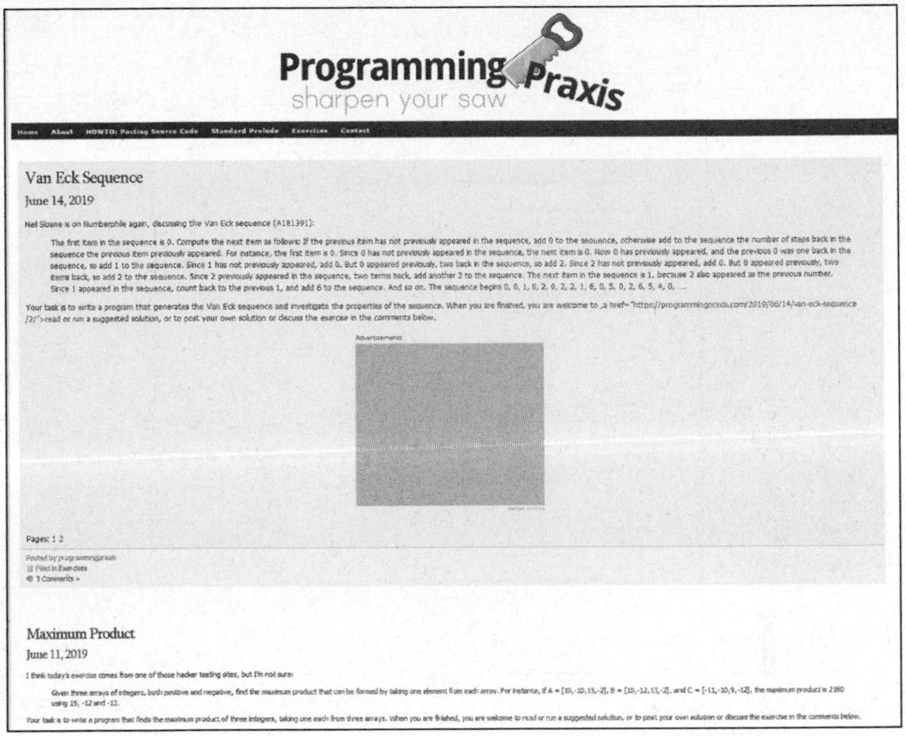

FIGURE 12-4: The latest puzzles appear in reverse chronological order on the Programming Praxis website.

Source: `https://programmingpraxis.com`

Topcoder

Topcoder (`www.topcoder.com`) bills itself as a crowdsourcing software development platform, but it's also a place where you can compete with other Topcoder users to solve challenges for real clients and get real money. When you click the Compete on Topcoder button on the Topcoder website's home page, the list of challenges appears, as shown in Figure 12-5.

Each challenge title contains a color-coded box to the left of the title: blue for web design and green for coding. You can view total amount of money being offered (not the total amount if you win) by clicking the challenge title name in the list.

After you click the title name, you'll see the Challenge Summary web page that tells you about the challenge and how much money will be awarded to the first, second, and third place finishers the Topcoder judges select. Some challenges reward all the money to the first person to create a working solution.

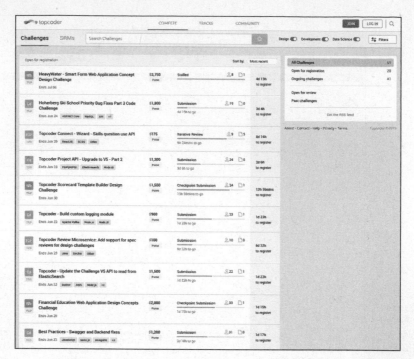

Source: www.topcoder.com

FIGURE 12-5:
The most recent
challenges
appear in the
Open for
Registration
section at the top
of the list.

MindCipher

The MindCipher website (www.mindcipher.com) shows a list of brain teaser puzzles in a wide variety of topics, including computer programming, as you see in Figure 12-6. To the right of each puzzle title and brief description, you see a graphic that tells you if MindCipher users find the puzzle easy, doable, or hard.

View the entire puzzle description in the Description web page by clicking the title of the puzzle; you see the full description as well as the Show Answer link below the description. When you click Show Answer, the answer appears below the link.

TIP

The description web page also shows solutions and questions by readers in the Comments section underneath the question, so you may need to train yourself to look only at the comments. If you want to comment on the site and/or rate the problem's difficulty, you have to create a MindCipher account to log into or you can log in with your Facebook account.

FIGURE 12-6:
View puzzles in a particular category by clicking a tag button within the Popular Tags list on the right side of the web page.

Source: www.mindcipher.com

4

Sealing the Deal

Learn how to manage multiple interviews.

Understand why you may (or may not) get the job.

Learn how to be clear-eyed about your pay and benefits as you enter negotiations with the company.

Manage the negotiation process so you know what cards to keep hidden, how to negotiate salary and other important stuff, and when to walk away from the table.

IN THIS CHAPTER

» **Managing multiple interviews**

» **Understanding when a company may contact you and how to follow up**

» **Learning what to do when a company rejects or doesn't contact you**

» **Negotiating the best deal**

» **Being clear about your health, time off, and retirement benefits**

Chapter **13**

Closing the Deal

You may have been so focused preparing for the interview that once it's over you may not know what to do with yourself. In some cases, you won't have to wait long as the company may ask you back for at least one more interview either on another day or even on the same day as your main interview. We start this chapter telling you about what to do if you receive multiple requests for interviews that companies all want to schedule around the same time. Then we tell you about the different types of interviews you may have with one company and how to manage each one.

Next, we move on to the post-interviews portion of your experience by explaining how long it may take for a company to get back to you. We also explain why it's not a bad idea for you to follow up on a regular basis to the point where you become such a pest that the company representative will have no choice but to give you some information.

If all your hard work doesn't pay off and you don't get the job, we talk about what to do then, and what to do if you don't get a response. You also learn how to contact the company to get information about why the dice came up snake eyes in a way that will help you improve your performance when you interview at your next prospective employer.

However, if you get a job offer, then we discuss how to accept the offer properly and what you need to know about negotiating your salary over the phone. We end the chapter by talking about understanding the benefits package the company offers including health coverage, time-off policies, 401(k) matching, and retirement benefits.

Scheduling Interviews with Multiple Companies

You probably haven't applied to only one company and put all your efforts into getting that *one* job. More likely, you've applied for several jobs; therefore, you shouldn't be surprised if you get requests for job interviews that companies all want to schedule around the same time. What to do?

There is no specific recommendation we can give because everyone is different. However, you should ask yourself some questions when you get an offer to interview:

>> Is this job in the place you want to live, whether it's in your current location or somewhere else?

>> Do you prefer working for a bigger or smaller company, and does this company fit the bill?

>> Do you want to wait to get a call for an interview from your dream company?

>> Will the company pay for you to come interview, or will you have to drive or fly out to the company's headquarters for one or more in-person interviews on your dime?

>> Are the company representatives who want to interview you flexible with their schedules because they know candidates likely have other interviews?

TIP

That last question may be the most important one because you should have at least a few days between each interview if at all possible. This strategy will not only give you a chance to relax and reflect on your last interview, it will also minimize your being unprepared at your next interview.

Managing Multiple Interviews with the Same Company

Earlier in this book, we talk about two interviews you'll likely have with a company: the phone screen (see Chapter 7) and the in-person interview that will include programming tests (see Chapter 8; we cover those tests in Chapters 8 through 12). With those two interviews out of the way, all you have to do is wait for the company representatives to make up their minds, right?

The answer is a definite maybe. The type of company you're interviewing with largely influences how many interviews you will have.

Knowing the types of interviews you may have

If you're interviewing with a startup company, you may not have a phone screen interview. Instead, a company representative will ask you to come to the company's headquarters to talk with the founders and/or the existing programming team in person. The startup may even hire you after the interview is over because it needs someone to start right away to help meet an important deadline.

In other cases, you may have more than two interviews because they want to know that you're not just good at programming — they want to hire you for the long term and want to make sure you're the right fit not just for the culture of the team but also for the company as a whole.

If the company is big enough to pay for a round-trip flight to its headquarters and perhaps pay for a hotel room, too, it's going to keep you there for as short a time as possible — likely no more than two days. So, expect to receive a schedule from a company representative (probably someone from human resources) that will include at least one entire day chock-full of interviews.

These interviews may include a panel interview that we talk about in Chapter 8 as well as interviews with people in different departments. The people you meet will likely include other software developers on the team you'd work with, as well as

>> developers on one or more other teams you would work with;

>> the hiring manager, department manager, and/or team manager; and

>> one or more people from the HR department.

You may have a second, partial day of interviews, and some of them may be with people who interviewed you the day before. (Then you get to have more fun at the airport. Yay.)

Meeting the team to see if you're a good fit

REMEMBER

When you meet people at the company, the company is evaluating you — and vice versa. You're evaluating them to find out if this is a company you want to work for. The people you interview with reflect the company's culture that will influence your life for potentially years to come.

If one or more employees expose a negative company culture, you need to recognize it right away and remove yourself from the interview as quickly and as politely as possible, no matter how large or small the company is.

For example, you may encounter a particularly nasty interviewer who is not only arrogant but just treats you badly. That person may be a fellow coworker on your team or could even be the team or department manager. You would likely suspect this person is acting this way toward you because he's threatened by your skills, the fact that someone else joining the team will diminish his position, or both. Either way, you probably wouldn't want to pursue a job there because that person can affect your work environment and your fate at the company to a large degree.

Grasping what you'll work on with the team

When you're being interviewed, you'll also have an opportunity to ask individual interviewers or groups of interviewers questions about the position. For example:

>> What kind of project will I be working on?

>> What kind of technology will I be using?

>> What's the software I'll be developing?

>> How will I be working with the team?

>> Who will my boss and coworkers be?

TIP

Asking questions of your interviewers gives you two advantages. The first is that you're showing interest in the job, and a lot of interviewers will be glad that you're not only interested in the job, but also that you're interested in working for the company.

More important, the answers you receive may compel you to ask more questions to get the answer to your primary question: Should you take this job?

For example, if you're interviewing for a job as a C# programmer, but the interviewers tell you that you'll maintain an old Visual Basic 6 application for legacy customers, then you'll want to ask more questions about why they're hiring for a C# programmer. That could lead to awkwardness for them, but clarity for you.

Learning about your future path with the company

Another important question to ask every interviewer is about your future path with the company. That is, you should ask, "What are my avenues for advancement?" Every employee you talk to should have an answer based on his or her own experiences that should inform your ability to grow your skills and compensation with the company over time . . . or not.

REMEMBER

If you're going to be relocating to a new city to take a job at this company, this question is *very* important because you could not only be working at the company, but also living in the city for a significant chunk of your life.

Some companies won't have much of an advancement plan — if it has one at all. For example, members of a startup company probably haven't given any thought to advancement plans because they're too busy trying to meet the next product deadline so they can land the next round of investor money.

Other companies, especially larger ones, may have specific tracks for developing yourself as far as your abilities will take you. For example, we remember that in the past, Hewlett-Packard had a technical track where people could continue to add to and improve their technical skills without any limits. Google also offers opportunities to change your career path if you feel that you've reached your limit in your current job and you're interested in doing something else.

Understanding When a Company May Contact You

Once you've finished the interview process with a company, it's easy to become impatient after a day or three — especially if you needed a job yesterday. The impatient mindset can help or hurt you.

It can hurt if you don't understand that the company may not contact you for a week, two weeks, or even a month. Even so, if a company representative doesn't reconnect with you after a week, then it's time to put your impatience to work and contact the company to ask for an update about the job.

Following up will not lose you the job

It's easy to feel that calling and following up will only serve to annoy your potential employer, perhaps so much so that the company representative you talk to will tell you that your call has cost you the job. If that happens, thank that person, because he helped you avoid working in a bad company culture.

When you do follow up, be sure to be polite every time and talk naturally, not formally or in a threatening manner. For example, you can say, "Hello again. I just wanted to touch base and see where you're at. I'm really excited about the opportunity about potentially working for you. And if you need any other information from me, please let me know and I'll send it right away."

The company may be pleasantly surprised that you're showing a high degree of interest and that you're also a person who follows through. The old, trite saying applies: The squeaky wheel gets the grease.

Being annoying can work for you

Don't just be content with the person you talk to saying not to worry and that he'll call you soon. When that person doesn't call you after a couple of days, call again and ask if there's any progress. Not only will company representatives not forget about you, they may even say among themselves, "Wow, this person's a go-getter who follows up and takes action, and so we'd better hire her before one of our competitors does."

You can also use a follow-up call or email message to update your potential employer about projects you're working on. For example, you can say, "Hey, I'm just checking in to let you know that I finished a new app, I wrote a new blog post about your industry, and I produced a new video that shows how I solved a problem that was bugging me. If you want to know what I'm up to, here's where to find all that new information."

What's more, your call can include follow-up information about topics you talked about during the interview, such as "At the interview we were talking about the problem your team is facing. I thought about it some more and I have some ideas, and here's what I'm thinking and what I'm reading online. I thought this might be helpful."

In sum, you're providing value beyond the interview, showing you want to be involved with the company, as well as being less annoying and more useful.

Coming Up Snake Eyes

All of your efforts preparing for the interviews, going through the interview process, and following up may result in the company . . . going in another direction. It's natural to feel disappointed, but there may be reasons you didn't get the job that have nothing to do with you.

In many cases, a job is given to someone ahead of time and the interview process was merely a formality. This happens more often in big companies where the law requires that human resources advertise a job externally and interview outside people. Unfortunately, you'll never know if that was the case because the company is under no obligation to tell you.

There are several other reasons why a company might refuse to give you an explanation about why you didn't get the job:

» Companies, especially bigger ones, don't want to risk being exposed violating one or more discrimination laws.

» The company doesn't want to say anything that you could dispute and take to civil and/or criminal court . . . or the media.

» You may see or hear news stories about workplace violence incidents from time to time, and some of those incidents stem from people who have been fired or didn't receive a job.

So, companies feel it's safest for the business and its employees to have a policy not to divulge any information to any job applicant who didn't receive an offer.

Receiving a generic response

If a company rep does give you an explanation, you'll probably get it in a generic letter or email message. You may even get a generic form letter in the mail that thanks you for your time, there were many qualified candidates, blah blah blah. What's more, the form letter probably won't invite you to contact them and the email message may have been sent by an automated account that no one can respond to.

Even so, that doesn't mean you shouldn't ask for an explanation. You may (should) still have the company business card or contact information that you picked up during your interview. That will give you an opportunity to contact the company by phone, email, or both.

You may also try to contact one of your interviewers and/or someone who works at the company either on a social media website like LinkedIn or even in person if you attend local developer meetings. However, don't expect much of a response from these people, either, as they likely know that if they give detailed information to rejected applicants then their own jobs may be in jeopardy.

REMEMBER

Get a hold of your emotions before you ask anyone at the company for more information. If you're angry or argumentative, expect a polite thank you and a quick phone hang-up, no response to your email message, the removal of your social media connection, or the other person walking away (and maybe other potential employers noticing) if you confront him or her in person.

Asking for more information

A better approach when you contact someone about why you weren't offered the job is to use it as an opportunity to improve for your next interview with another company. If the person you're talking to or emailing interviewed you or talked with you while you were at the company, start by thanking her for the opportunity to interview with the company. The next step is to say that you're trying to improve your skills and that you'd like one or more pointers so you can get better.

For example, you can say, "Is there just one thing that you saw that I can improve on? I'm not sensitive at all. I just honestly want to improve myself and could you give me one recommendation for doing that?"

This approach won't guarantee that you get the answers you seek. The other person may say that the company won't allow her to talk with any applicants about the job. In that case, you have to thank her and let it go. But you need to ask, because the other person may be receptive to that kind of question and it may lead to a productive conversation.

TIP

If you receive valuable feedback about what you can improve, incorporate what you learn into the next mock interview. Ask your mock interviewers if they notice your improvements if they don't mention it on their own. If they don't notice, you have more work to do. If they do, then the real interviewers will, too. (You can read more about the mock interview process in Chapter 8.)

Receiving Your Offer

Congratulations! Your hard work has paid off and you've received a job offer. It may not have come from the first company you interviewed with, but that just made you stronger and now you're . . . well, hold your horses. You still need to know what the offer is so you can start preliminary negotiations to try to get the best deal for you.

Getting the word

You'll probably get a verbal offer by phone first. The person making the offer may be the manager of the team, the manager of the department, or the hiring manager.

When you get a verbal offer, ask the company representative on the other end to wait so you can get a pad and paper (or can type on your preferred computing device). When you're ready, write down or type everything the rep tells you and then repeat what he said to ensure that you both understand what the terms of the offer are.

If you haven't received the offer in an email message, then it's important that you negotiate the offer while you're on the phone, as we explain shortly.

Obtaining a written offer

If the company person on the other line has told you that you'll receive email with the offer, check your inbox and your junk email folder to find out if you've received it. If you haven't received it, ask the company representative if you'll receive it during the call.

Though a written offer in email isn't binding, it's a good opportunity for you to compare what the email message says and what the company representative told you over the phone. If you don't receive that emailed offer, then you can proceed to negotiate the offer on the phone based on what you and the company representative mutually understand is that offer.

Negotiating the offer over the phone

You may be afraid to negotiate the offer because you think showing any dissatisfaction with the offer will lead the company to withdraw it and hang up. If a company actually does that, then this is another opportunity for you to celebrate not having to work in a terrible company culture.

Before you receive a written offer on paper, it's good to use this opportunity to start the negotiation process and try to raise your offer. For example, the team manager has called you to say, "We'd like to hire you for the job, we're willing to offer you $85,000 a year, and we'll give you a written offer when you come over. When can we get together?"

This is the time to respond with a counteroffer by saying something like, "That's great. I'm really excited. That amount does seem a little bit low, though. I'm wondering what we can do here to make this a better opportunity because I have some other opportunities that I'm considering."

The team manager may not want to show her cards yet . . . or she doesn't have the authority to negotiate over the phone. She may say something like, "We can meet in person and talk about that when we talk in person. When would you like to get together?" At that point, you can set up your appointment.

WARNING

Don't forget to bring your phone meeting notes to the formal negotiating meeting. You may find that the written offer has different terms than what you and the company rep discussed over the phone. For example, the salary may differ between what you were offered on the phone and the printed formal offer letter, and that will likely be your first topic of discussion.

Knowing when pay is not the top consideration

The person you're talking to on the phone may not be willing to talk with you about anything other than your salary. Indeed, your salary may not be the top consideration because the company will offer other benefits including medical plans, 401(k) plans, other retirement plans, and time off for a certain amount of time during the calendar year.

A company may present you with a formal offer that shows that the salary is lower than you'd like, but also shows you that the cash value of the benefits means your job will have a combined value that's worth your consideration. You'll have to decide if you want to negotiate the entire package with the company, and we talk more about honing your negotiation skills in Chapter 14.

REMEMBER

After you negotiate the offer, you'll get a formal written offer that you'll be asked to sign. However, if you haven't started your employment yet, be aware that the company can withdraw a signed, written offer at any time.

Being Clear about Your Benefits

Speaking of benefits, if you're offered a full-time, salaried position, benefits are what a company uses to entice you to sign the agreement. After all, contract jobs don't usually come with benefits.

As we said earlier, some companies will give you a monetary value of the benefits they're giving you. However, most companies are likely to just give you the list of benefits and let you decide what they're worth to you. It's likely you won't see these benefits until you receive the formal offer letter and you can hammer out the details with the company reps.

The good news is that you can negotiate these benefits as part of your overall compensation package, but before you learn how to do that in Chapter 14, you need to understand the benefits the company has offered you.

Understanding the company's health plans

Ralph Waldo Emerson said, "The first wealth is health," and health plans belong at the top of your benefits list. No matter if your health plan benefits are paid 100 percent by the company or you have to pay a copayment for some costs (like prescription medications), the health plan is considered part of your overall salary because the company is paying part of that salary toward keeping your vim and vigor every day.

As you look at the company's health plan, you should look at the value of the benefit and how much you would use. For example, if the company is paying for a $5,000 per month medical plan, but you only need $500 to $1,000 per month, the difference isn't worth much to you. But if that $5,000 per month also includes dental and vision plans that are paid for by the company 100 percent, then you may be more amenable to the company's plan.

The company may also provide a medical plan that gives you the option of selecting a plan that's right for you. Some plans give you different options with different deductibles and others give you more flexible "cafeteria-style" plans that let you pick and choose which services you need.

You need to take your time to review these plans carefully during your meeting with the company. If you feel you need more time to review your options, ask the company people you meet with if they'll let you take the plans home to chew on them and give them an answer the next day.

TIP

When you review these plans, you need to take the time to run three different scenarios in your head: the nothing happens scenario, the scenario where you get an average number of medical bills for something that happened (like breaking your arm), and the worst-case scenario where you become seriously ill or injured. Then you can crunch the numbers and find out how much you want to pay each month (if the company offers subsidized monthly payments) and how high you want your deductible to be.

Matching your 401(k) benefits

Your company will likely offer 401(k) retirement plan benefits and offer to match the contribution that will be deducted from your salary automatically so you grow your nest egg more quickly.

How quickly is something that the company should tell you, such as the maximum amount it'll match every month. You also need to ask the company representatives the following important questions:

» What is the maximum the company can contribute?

» Will the percentage the company matches be affected if you roll over your existing 401(k) to your new employer?

» How much does the maximum percentage equate to dollars flowing into your 401(k) account every year?

You need to ask yourself some questions, too. Do you plan to (or think you will) borrow from your 401(k) account at some point? If you are, then the 401(k) may be worth it to you as a source of funding when you need it, such as to address a family emergency.

If you plan to use your 401(k) as a long-term investment for your retirement, then you need to ask yourself if the matching amount is a worthwhile addition to your benefits package.

Learning how much time off you get

We're human beings and we all need some degree of downtime, though some people need more convincing of that fact than others. So, the company needs to clearly spell out how much time off you'll get.

There are a lot of questions about what "time off" really means to the company, so take the time to understand and negotiate how the company approaches time off, including:

>> Is this time off for vacation, sick leave, or both?

>> If the time off is only for vacation, how much time do you get for sick leave?

>> Is sick leave only for you, or does it cover taking time off to take care of someone in your family as well?

>> How long in advance do you have to declare that you're going to take time off?

>> What happens if you have an emergency, such as to manage a medical issue in your family, and you need to take time off right away?

>> What's the company's holiday schedule, and are holidays exempt from your allotment of time off?

>> Does time off apply to days before or after holidays, such as the day after Thanksgiving in the United States?

>> If you have to work one or both days during a weekend to meet an important deadline, are those day(s) added to your allotment of time off for the year?

>> If you take less than your allotment of time off during the year, are you paid that amount at the beginning of the following year, or does that vacation time roll over and is added to the time off you're entitled to during the following year?

These are just some of the questions to get you started. Your own personal situation and the company's flexibility may also prompt you to ask some of your own questions, such as how often you can work from home and how doing so affects your allotment of time off.

REMEMBER

You need to quantify the pay you would receive if you didn't take that time off. This is especially important to know if you opt not to take time off because you're the type who gets bored after being on vacation for a day or if you find you work most, if not all, of the year to meet one or several important deadlines.

Retiring with benefits

You should also know what other benefits you'll get, or you need to ask about them during your negotiation period. (Full disclosure: This information is explained by Debbie Downer.)

First, you need to know if there are any retirement benefits and if there are any restrictions that come with those benefits. If retirement benefits don't kick in until 20 years of service, and you're either going to reach retirement age in 15 years or you expect to be doing something else within 5 years, then those benefits are worthless.

Retirement benefits may include a pension if you're working for a company that's big enough to offer one. Pensions are also largely meaningless if you're not going to use them for years. What's more, the company may not be around to pay them by the time you retire. If they are, there's no guarantee that the company will have enough money to offer either the pension amount they originally promised or any pensions at all.

Finally, you should also ask if there will be any stock compensation and when any vesting of the stock will take place. If a company already has stock, then receiving stock is obviously more valuable than if a company doesn't know when it will go public and the vesting date is only within a vague future time frame.

The sad trombone reality is that in most cases, retirement and stock benefits don't count toward your benefits package because any retirement or stock compensation doesn't guarantee you any income now or in the future.

Chapter **14**

Honing Your Negotiating Skills

A company's job offer is just that — an offer. It's one that you can and must negotiate if you want to get the best benefits package. If you decide you'd rather be grateful that you're getting an offer and not negotiate, you'll not only leave a lot of money on the table, but also you may be seen as being a weaker person, which won't help you in your daily work life.

As a job candidate who negotiates your entire benefits package, you will command respect within the company, because you'll show that you're not afraid to fight for what you want and you're not afraid to get into confrontations and win them, which is an important life skill in general. In the work environment, you need to show these skills to deal effectively with customers, team members, and higher-ups in the company.

In sum, if you're a yes-person and accept whatever you're going to take, don't be surprised if you'll be asked to do everything other team members don't want to do and be passed up for promotions and higher salaries.

This chapter helps you hone your negotiating skills as you deal with the company to get the best deal, just as card players strategize to get the winning hand. If you prefer Go Fish, poker, or bridge, the concept is still the same no matter your preferred card game.

We start by telling you where you should do your research online to find out what the salary ranges are for similar programming jobs in the area where you may work and learn what programmers with your proposed job title are earning. That information will inform you about how much you think you're worth in terms of salary and other benefits, such as time off.

Once you have your expectations set, you need to know what cards to keep hidden, and when the time is right to reveal them. That is, you don't want to blurt out your desired salary and benefits when company representatives ask for them. You need to engage in a series of offers and counteroffers with company representatives to settle on a final benefits package that you and the company are happy with.

Next, you learn what not to do, including negotiating over just your salary and not your entire benefits package. You also learn why you shouldn't pit the job offer against other job offers no matter if they're real or if you're bluffing.

Finally, you learn when it's the right time to fold your cards, get up, and walk away from the table, and how to do so professionally.

Finding Information from Employees Online

It's common in job interviews for at least one interviewer to ask you questions about your current job including the big one: how much money you're making. It's important as you start your negotiations to have the upper hand and not reveal current salary information that could foil your ability to get the benefits you want from your potential new employer.

Therefore, before you start negotiating, you should find information about employee salaries and what employees think about working for those companies on websites that offer that information. Employee reviews may include salary information that you can use and the bonus reward of knowing what you may expect when you start working at the company.

TIP

We've listed three of the most popular employee salary and/or review sites on the web, but there are many others. If you type **glassdoor competitors** into Google, you'll not only see a list of competitors but also a message thread on Quora that contains suggestions for finding salary and/or employee review sites both in the United States and other countries.

Glassdoor

Glassdoor (www.glassdoor.com), shown in Figure 14-1, is the most popular and best known website for obtaining salary information and for reading reviews from employees about companies they worked or currently work for.

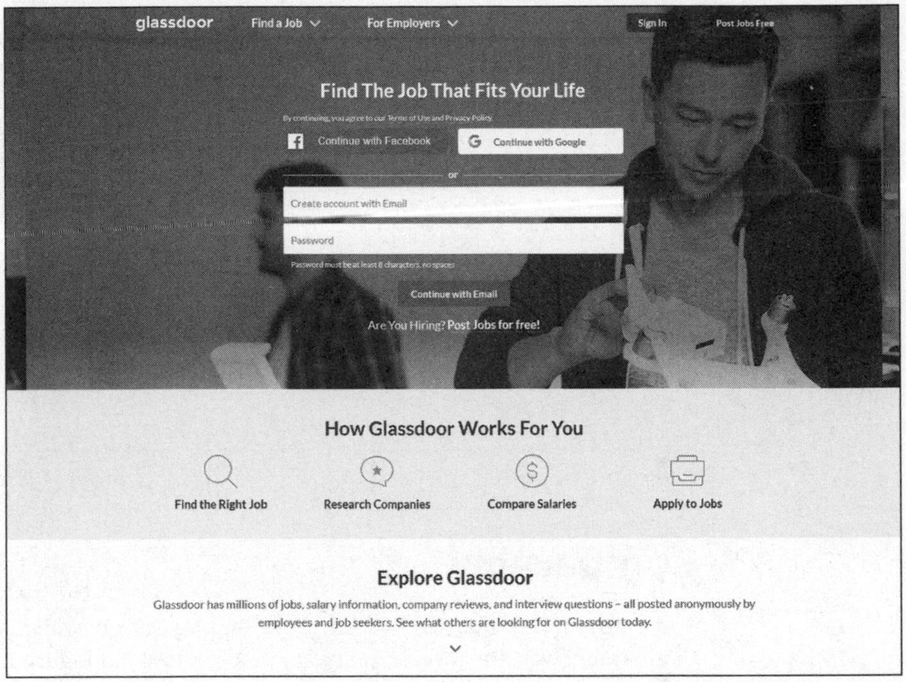

Source: www.glassdoor.com

FIGURE 14-1: The Glassdoor website allows you to log in with your Facebook or Google account.

You don't even have to go to the Glassdoor website to find information about the specific company you're looking for. In Google, type **glassdoor** followed by the name of the company and the company office location and then press Enter.

For example, if you type **Glassdoor HPE Roseville**, you'll see a list of reviews for the Hewlett-Packard Enterprise facility in Roseville, California. The entry at the top of the results list shown in Figure 14-2 has the link to the reviews page on Glassdoor as well as the aggregated rating for the company based on one (bad) to five (great) stars.

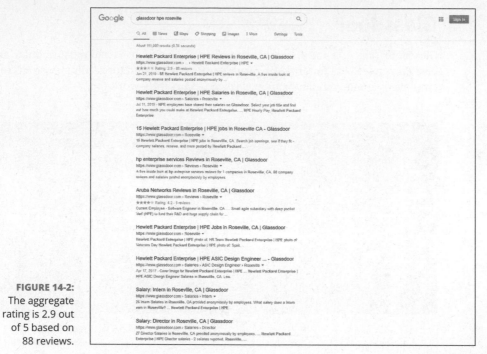

FIGURE 14-2:
The aggregate
rating is 2.9 out
of 5 based on
88 reviews.

Comparably

You can quickly find the overall score employees give their employers on the Comparably website (www.comparably.com), shown in Figure 14-3.

All you have to do on the Comparably site is type the name of the company you want to search in the Search box and then press Enter. A list of search results appears on the results page.

Open the results page by clicking the company name or associated photo in the results list. The culture score appears prominently on the company page, and the score is ranked using the classroom scale of A+ to F. For example, Figure 14-4 shows that Google gets a ranking of A+.

TIP

You can also learn about salaries for a specific job title in a specific city by clicking Salaries in the menu bar at the top of every web page on the site. Then you can add the specific job title and postal ZIP code to find the average salary for that area.

Source: www.comparably.com

FIGURE 14-3:
You need to
sign up for a
Comparably
account to use all
its features.

Source: www.comparably.com

FIGURE 14-4:
The Comparably
results for Google
also show CEO
Sundar Pichai has
an 81 percent
favorability score.

This information is useful to find out if that average will give you enough money to live comfortably in the city where you work, or if you'll have to live in a more affordable area and commute daily. If the average won't work for you, you'll need to increase your planned salary offer accordingly.

CareerBliss

The CareerBliss website (www.careerbliss.com) allows you to find jobs, research salaries in your area, and read company reviews, as shown in Figure 14-5. One interesting feature of CareerBliss is that it compiles an annual list of the 50 happiest companies in the United States based on tens of thousands of employee reviews.

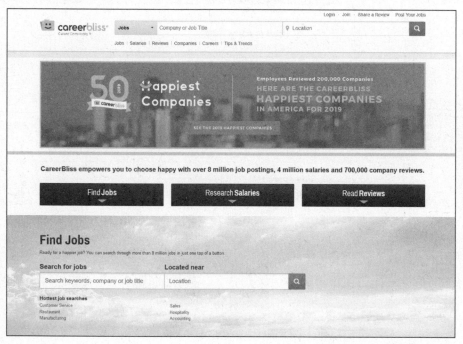

FIGURE 14-5:
Click one of the black buttons to find jobs, research salaries, or read employee reviews of companies.

Source: www.careerbliss.com

You can also search for salaries by job title if you want to get a more general idea of what companies are paying people like you. Type the company name in the Search box to get more specific information.

What's more, you can search for companies in the Read Company Reviews section on the home page. In the results page, you can view the number of reviews and the aggregated scores based on a 1 (bad) to 5 (great) star scale. Read individual reviews by clicking the number of reviews to the right of the star icons, such as "160 Reviews."

If someone at the company is a friend of yours and/or you've built up a good rapport with one or more employees at the company, you may want to ask them about the salary ranges . . . but only if you do that delicately. Bluntly asking people how much they make may put them in an awkward spot and they may not even be allowed to divulge that information.

Instead, ask if the pay for the department you may be working in is within a certain range. For example, you can ask, "Is the pay in the department somewhere between $80,000 and $100,000?" If they respond with a definite answer, you can follow up by asking if the starting pay is at the upper or lower end of the scale. This approach may not get you anywhere, but it's worth a try if your friend or potential colleague can provide a ballpark figure because then you've added another valuable card to your hand.

Dealing with Company Salary Information and Expectations

Now that you've done your research and you have your cards ready, the company will try to get you to at least ante up if not reveal one or more cards. One way companies do this is by bluntly asking, "What is your current salary?" You may receive a less blunt but similar question; for example, Salesforce asks, "What is the compensation you expect?"

You may feel no matter how the company asks you questions about salary, it's perfectly reasonable to answer them, and so it feels uncomfortable not to divulge this information. However, doing so will put you at a disadvantage.

Learning the company's cards

The company representatives already have an advantage because they've researched salary information — probably more than you have — and they also know what they're paying their own employees. So, they want to use one of three strategies to pay you as little salary as possible when you start your job:

>> They want to get a number from you and then give you a slightly higher offer so it looks like they're being generous.

>> If you give the company representatives a salary amount that's on the lower end of their wage scale, or a number that's even lower than the wage scale because you haven't done your homework, then they'll offer that lower amount. If you discover later that you should have asked for a higher amount and you try to negotiate a higher wage, the company representatives will claim the wage they've offered is in line with your expectations.

>> If you answer with a number that's too high, the company may not want to pay you that much money . . . at least not right away. If you can't negotiate a lower salary to start and work up to the salary you're looking for over time — that is, if the company is even willing to negotiate — then the company will walk away from the table.

Keeping your cards close to your vest

So, the name of this negotiation game is that the person who offers the amount first loses, and it's important that the company gives you the first offer. Company representatives know this, too, and that's why they'll be so insistent on asking you some variant of "What are you looking for?"

You can politely answer these salary-related questions in one of several ways depending on your feel of the situation:

>> I would rather not talk about that right now.

>> I can't reveal that amount because it's proprietary information from my current employer.

>> I'd rather not reveal that information because I think it would put me in a disadvantage.

>> I don't want to reveal that information because I don't see how it's relevant to the job you're hiring me for.

>> I prefer to discuss salary and other benefits when we decide we're going to work together.

>> I have a full benefits package and salary is just one part of it, so the salary part by itself doesn't give me enough context to be used in any kind of evaluation or negotiation.

>> I'll consider any reasonable offer.

Forcing your hand

TIP

If someone from human resources or your potential boss insists on salary information to move on, then based on the homework you did finding salary information online, it's best to give a salary range that's at the higher end of your expectations.

Then the company will finally give you an offer that will likely be at the low end of that range, but at least you can still negotiate the price higher because now the company representatives know the range they're working with.

Managing the Negotiation Process

Once the company gives you a salary amount or benefits package to consider, you need to give a counteroffer — even if the company's offer gives you more than what you expected.

Why? A company that's invested enough time and effort to interview you and make an offer is always going to come up a little bit low and leave itself a little bit of wiggle room to negotiate.

TIP

Always presume the company is experienced with negotiating with potential employees and will expect you to provide a counteroffer that's a little bit higher. You don't want to leave any money on the table just like you wouldn't knowingly leave a public place without your wallet that has a couple thousand dollars in it.

Giving a counteroffer

You may be afraid to negotiate because you think you're going to lose the job, especially if this is the job you dreamed of or you need a job right now.

Here's our counteroffer for your brain: You need to understand who's the most important person in the conversation. (Yes, you.) If you're still not convinced, we recommend you read the book, *Never Split the Difference* by Chris Voss and Tahl Raz (HarperBusiness). After you read it, you'll understand why Voss and Raz subtitled the book, *Negotiating as If Your Life Depended on It* — because it does.

It's also natural to think that if you counteroffer with a number that you think the company will see as too high, then it's more acceptable to meet in the middle of what the company has offered and what your desired highest salary is. Then the company representative will counteroffer with an amount that's lower than what you think the middle is. Congratulations! You've just lost a lot of money.

So, counteroffer with your high amount. The company representative likely expects that, too, because he expects your counteroffer will come with a little wiggle room, and you'll be willing to accept a somewhat lower salary than your counteroffer amount. In the worst-case scenario, the company representative won't negotiate and will say that the offer is final. Then you'll have to review the rest of the company's proposed benefits package and see if you can negotiate one or more of those benefits.

REMEMBER

Making counteroffers and getting more money won't just improve your life and livelihood right now, but also in the future as you grow with the company. After all, you expect to get raises at some point, so you need to remember that raises are usually based on the percentage of your pay. If your pay is higher, then your raises will be higher, too. What's more, if you're going to get another job in the future, then the higher pay from your current job will likely lead to an even higher starting salary at your new job.

Negotiating more than salary

The first negotiation session is usually about salary, but that's only one of the cards in the company's hand. The rest have to do with other benefits the company is offering. These benefits could offset a lower salary if you get more flexibility in your job and more opportunities for making a lot of money if you think those opportunities will come in a reasonable amount of time.

For example, you can make counteroffers about a signing bonus for joining the company, the amount of time off you get, the 401(k) matching amount, and how many shares of company stock you get.

There may be other options in the package to negotiate. If the company is a startup, you may be able to negotiate an ownership stake when the company meets clear financial milestones.

You could negotiate your roles and responsibilities. If there's the opportunity to work from home, you can negotiate how often you can do that. You can even negotiate the equipment the company will provide you to get your job done.

Avoiding pitting companies against each other

It's possible you'll be negotiating with one company knowing that you already have one or more offers from other companies. This is one card you don't want to play because it makes it very easy for the company to withdraw its offer.

So, play it straight. Don't respond to the company's offer by saying, "Hey, I got a higher offer from another company that has also offered me a job." The company representatives will likely ask you what that offer is.

Tell them and they'll counteroffer with a slightly higher offer than what the other company is offering, and you'll be prevented from getting the highest amount possible. If you don't, and they have to guess, then one of two things may happen.

First, you may get a much higher offer than what you were expecting, but they'll still get a bad vibe about you and they may not be as willing to negotiate other parts of your benefits package. Worse, people in the company will talk about it, and you don't want to come into a new job with people giving you the side eye.

The other result is that they'll see you as unprofessional and possibly lying to them, withdraw their offer, thank you for your interest, and escort you from the building.

If you want to mention that you're entertaining multiple offers, you can do so at the end of the negotiation. You don't have to tell the company representatives about the other offers or even the companies' names because you should always presume that company recruiters talk to each other. That's especially true if you're looking for jobs in the same geographic area, and those recruiters can ensure you won't play cards with them anytime soon.

Walking away

The best negotiators are those who are willing and able to walk away. The company you're interviewing with is certainly willing to walk away if it can't get you to agree because it likely has second and third choices for the job.

The best way to look out for number one (yes, you) is to ensure that you're interviewing with multiple companies and, better yet, have at least one other offer from another company. If you've applied at a number of companies and interviewed well with at least a few of them, it's likely you'll have the ability to walk away from the company's table, too.

REMEMBER

What's more, you should have some side projects that you're working on so you're still generating income if you have to walk away. You don't want to be in a situation where the company you're negotiating with is the only one you've applied to and interviewed with. In that situation you'll be more desperate to take any offer whether you realize it or not.

If you decide to walk away, do so in a respectful way — don't be angry, threatening, or plain old nasty. (And we don't mean in a Janet Jackson sort of way.) You can say, "Hey, this isn't what I'm looking for. I'm sorry we couldn't come to an agreement, but this isn't the right opportunity for me. I'd love to work for you, and I'm sure we could do great things together, but we can't agree about the job benefits and that's okay."

Being polite and respectful will leave the company representatives still thinking highly of you — so much so that they may decide to continue negotiations. They may even offer you more because you're head and shoulders above their other choices, or their second and/or third choices don't work out.

What's more, one day in the future, this company may invite you to apply for a different job with you specifically in mind, which is the best kind of job offer to get. Then don't be surprised if you end up with a better hand than you had during your first card game.

5

The Part of Tens

Learn how to stand out to companies both online and in person.

Be prepared to answer non-technical questions a company may ask you during your phone screen and/or your interview.

Know how to create a proper résumé, dress correctly, and behave properly so your résumé doesn't end up in the round file.

Find resources for information that will give you a better chance of being hired by the company of your dreams.

IN THIS CHAPTER

» Having a professional headshot taken by a photographer

» Establishing a GitHub profile and get plenty of referrals

» Creating your own YouTube channel

» Having a good blog as well as produce an audio podcast and vlog

» Showing off mobile apps, a self-published book, and speaking engagements

Chapter **15**

Ten Ways to Stand Out

I f you're applying for a software development job, always presume that many of your fellow programmers will apply for that job, too. Here are ten ways you, and not just your résumé and cover letter, can stand out to your potential employer and get you an interview.

Have a Professional Headshot

Use a professional headshot, taken by a professional photographer, as your profile picture on all your social media profiles. Don't use a good selfie you took of yourself while you were on vacation. Instead, get some recommendations for a photographer from friends, colleagues, and even your social media connections.

Then dress professionally (at least from the waist up), get well-groomed, go to the photography studio, and get headshots that will show you're a professional. Once you get the photos and you've decided on the ones you want to use, put that headshot on all your social media profiles to create a consistent brand for yourself.

TIP

If you already use a professional photographer to take family portraits on occasion, here's a tip on how to save some money on a professional headshot. Gather the family to get some pictures done for relatives and ask the photographer if you could get a couple of headshots for yourself as well. You should already be professionally dressed and groomed, so an additional headshot or two of yourself will cost you little to nothing extra — probably the latter if you've been using your family photographer for a while.

Establish a GitHub Profile

If you don't have a GitHub profile to interact with other software developers, sign up for free on the GitHub website (`https://github.com`), shown in Figure 15-1.

FIGURE 15-1:
GitHub makes it easy for you to sign up for free.

A GitHub profile not only gets you access to other developers, it also affords you the opportunity to demonstrate your programming abilities. If one or more people who work at an employer can find your GitHub profile and can see the type of code you've written as well as the projects you've contributed to, they'll have much more confidence that:

>> You can write code.

>> You are a good coder.

>> You can actually do what you say you can do on your résumé.

REMEMBER

If you have a GitHub profile but you haven't worked on any projects there in a while, now is a good time to get more involved so you can make it as impressive to prospective employers (and other programmers) as you can.

Get Plenty of Referrals

One big benefit of LinkedIn is that you can get and ask for plenty of online referrals, which LinkedIn calls recommendations, and post them on your LinkedIn profile for anyone to see. But you shouldn't just rely on people to give you recommendations on LinkedIn — you should already have plenty of people you could ask who would be happy to recommend you for a programming job.

So, ask those people if one or more people will write you a recommendation letter to send with your cover letter and résumé. The hiring manager or team manager may be a bit confused at first with all the papers included in your envelope, but then realize that you have plenty of people who are happy to recommend you and talk with company management about you.

That added proof that you're well-regarded in the industry will get your résumé and cover letter noticed. Referrals are not a panacea because you still have to make sure your résumé and cover letter look great, but including referral letters will make it much more likely that whoever is reviewing résumés looks at yours.

TIP

You can show your appreciation by writing a recommendation letter of your own and send those to your friends and colleagues who recommend you. After all, your friends and colleagues may need recommendations for a job or other position they want.

Have a Video Résumé on Social Networking Sites

We live in an age where it's easy to make videos and post them online, so it's a good idea to post a video résumé starring you on all your social media websites.

You can hire a videographer to professionally produce your video résumé, but you can probably do it yourself using your webcam. Just be sure to practice talking naturally into the camera so you come off as authentic and genuine. When you're ready to record, we recommend men wear at least a shirt and tie (if you're just sitting down) and groom yourself so you look professional.

You can put a link to your video résumé in your printed one. When people reviewing your résumé type in the link, they should see a brief video that not only features you talking about who you are as a programmer and your experience, but also shows some of your personality so the viewer can get to know you a little bit.

If potential interviewers feel like you're someone they want to work with after they watch your video résumé, don't be surprised if you get a phone call or email message asking to set up a phone screen or an in-person interview.

TIP

You should shorten the link to your video résumé so people don't have to type in a long and complicated URL in their browser's address bar. One popular site for shortening a URL is Bitly at `https://bitly.com`.

Create Your Own YouTube Channel

If you want to go one step further with your videos and stand out not just to potential interviewers but to the software developer community at large, include your video résumé on your YouTube channel. This channel should also include several videos that show off your personality and expertise (see Figure 15-2).

A YouTube channel that you promote regularly on your other social media and software developer websites like GitHub will start to get you followers. What's more, people at your prospective employer will look at your YouTube channel and think, "Wow, this person is teaching hundreds of developers on YouTube, so this is a good person to have on our team. This is someone who not only knows their stuff but will help our other programmers learn and grow."

Your YouTube channel may not only attract followers but may also prompt people to send comments asking if you're looking for a job. If you decide to start looking for employment, you can create a video that says you're looking for a job and feature that video on your channel so you can generate leads.

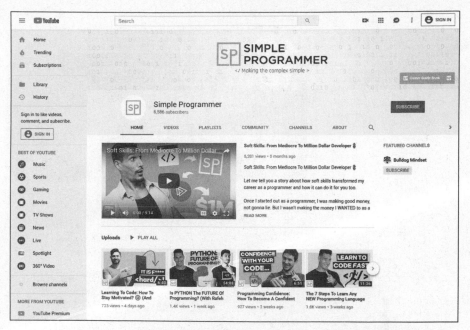

FIGURE 15-2:
The Simple Programmer website has numerous videos about a variety of programming topics.

Source: https://simpleprogrammer.com

Have a Good Blog to Show Your Expertise

Programming requires you to type code, so you should have a good blog that shows your coding expertise either in your preferred programming language and/or a variety of programming languages. A blog, such as the Simple Programmer blog shown in Figure 15-3, can

>> Include instructional articles about how to perform a task in a specific language;

>> Discuss tips, tricks, techniques, and trends in software development; and

>> Include articles from guest authors who talk about their areas of expertise.

If you design your blog so you feature your desired search keywords prominently and frequently, Google will have an easy time finding your blog when people search for those keywords. Don't forget to promote your latest blog posts on your social media and software developer websites, too.

FIGURE 15-3:
The Simple Programmer website has a blog with a number of articles written by different authors.

Source: https://simpleprogrammer.com

You may find that during the interview, one or more interviewers will ask you about the blog because they've been reading articles on it. So, the blog acts as an extended interview that shows people at your prospective employer that you write well, can articulate your points, and that you're an influencer and leader in the programming community.

WARNING

Update your blog regularly with new articles. If you haven't updated your blog even in a couple of months, your articles will start to look stale, and you'll give the impression to your interviewers that you're inattentive and don't follow through.

Produce a Podcast and/or Vlog

If you want to go all-out to promote your expertise and personality, then add an audio podcast or its video equivalent, the vlog (short for *video log*), to your blog and YouTube channel offerings.

The vlog can be posted to both your social media websites, your blog itself, and/or your YouTube channel. You may also want to have your podcast on sites that host podcasts, such as Libsyn (https://libsyn.com), shown in Figure 15-4.

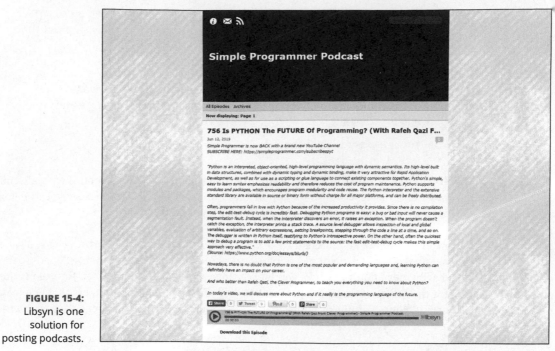

FIGURE 15-4:
Libsyn is one solution for posting podcasts.

Source: https://libsyn.com

If you're the host of a podcast, it's likely you won't talk during the entirety of each podcast. (The length of a podcast will vary depending on the topic.) Instead, you'll be talking with other people and creating a lot of connections. You'll also show that you're involved in the developer community.

As you build influence and a loyal listenership and/or viewership, you may become a celebrity among developers. Your popularity will make it easier for you to get the job you want because companies want to hire a famous software developer to work on their teams.

Point to Mobile Apps You've Already Developed in App Stores

If you've published one or more apps in an iOS or Android app store, don't forget to include this information in your résumé and cover letter, and ensure that any interviewers can easily find a link to the app on your social media profiles, blog, and YouTube channel.

Showing that you've developed one or more apps gives interviewers proof that:

>> You can write code just like your résumé says.

>> You can develop software through the entire life cycle from design to publication, which shows you can contribute to the programming team and the company.

>> You're a winner. (So go get a chicken dinner.)

If you haven't built an app before, there are plenty of tutorials online — all you have to do is type **build ios app** or **build android app** in Google and you'll get a results page full of tutorial links so you can get started.

TIP

After you create and publish an app, produce a "making of" video on your YouTube channel. This video should tell viewers about the app, how you developed it, the discoveries and drawbacks you had during development, and what your plans are for the future of the app. That last part will show potential employers that you take care of your customers and keep thinking of ways to make the app better for them.

Write and Self-Publish a Book

The one tangible thing you can bring with you to your interview, other than copies of your résumé, is a copy of a self-published book. It can be difficult to write books for major publishers unless you already have experience with them as a technical editor, you coauthor a book with a lead author, or if you've self-published a book.

It's easier than ever to publish and distribute a self-published book. You can sell your book as an ebook on websites including Amazon and Barnes & Noble as well as publish printed copies to give to people and sell on Amazon. The wikiHow website shown in Figure 15-5 (www.wikihow.com/Self-Publish-a-Book) gives you step-by-step instructions about how to write and publish your own book.

A book can make you a little bit of money, especially if you take the time to study successful self-published authors — for example, look at Andy Weir, who self-published the novel *The Martian*. More important, the book serves as an advertisement for your services that shows interviewers that:

>> You committed the time, money, and effort to write and publish a book.

>> You're a published authority on a given topic because not very many developers have self-published a book (though one coauthor of this book has).

>> You have writing skills, which could help you make more money in your new job if you're a technical writer as well as a programmer.

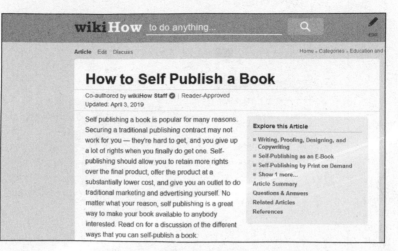

FIGURE 15-5:
Scroll down the wikiHow web page to view all the steps you need to take to self-publish a book.

REMEMBER

After you publish the book, don't forget to promote it not only in your cover letter and list it in your résumé, but also on all your online media and social networking websites. What's more, if you have the book listed on Amazon, then include a shortened URL link to the book page so interviewers can see it; the interviewers will appreciate a short URL to type because Amazon page URLs are almost as long as lines to get on popular Disneyland rides.

Speak at Developer and Business Events

You may not have thought about speaking at events, or maybe you don't want to think of it because the fear of public speaking, or glossophobia, is considered by some (perhaps including you) to be worse than death.

If you want to get up the courage to speak but don't know where to get training, go to the Toastmasters International website (www.toastmasters.org) and find a club in your area by clicking the Find a Club button in the upper-right corner of the screen. Then search for your nearest club in the Find a Club web page shown in Figure 15-6.

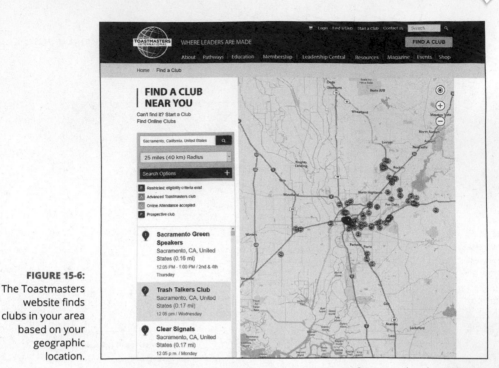

FIGURE 15-6:
The Toastmasters website finds clubs in your area based on your geographic location.

Source: www.toastmasters.org

Toastmasters International is considered the premier organization for professionals to learn how to speak effectively and become better leaders. After you select your club, you can attend a meeting for free if there are no current restrictions to joining a club. (Some clubs have restrictions and the website will tell you if that's so.) Once you decide to join, you can sign up as a new member for only $65 as of this writing; renewals cost $45 per year.

It may take you some time to get yourself where you want to be as a speaker, but once you gain enough confidence, you can start looking for speaking opportunities at local or regional events.

Check with Meetup events for software developers in your local area and ask the event coordinator about speaking opportunities. The same goes for local chamber of commerce and/or Rotary club meetings, though you'll probably have to produce a different presentation for those business-oriented audiences.

TIP

No matter where you speak, you'll likely have members of companies in the audience who may be impressed with you. After your presentation, one or more people may ask for your card so you can speak to their employees and/or recommend you as a speaker for a large developer conference (so make sure you have business cards with you!). Some people may be so impressed with your leadership abilities that they'll ask you if you're looking for a job.

REMEMBER

Before your speaking engagement, ask the event coordinator if you can record your presentation on video. Then you can make that video available for wider viewing later on your social media and/or online media websites. A large developer conference may record all speakers on video and give you the URL to the conference website so you can include a link to your presentation online as well as in your résumé and cover letter.

Chapter **16**

Ten Non-Technical Questions You May Be Asked

Your phone screen and/or in-person interview will likely include some non-technical questions — better known as ones designed to test your "soft skills." You need to prepare for these questions ahead of time because if any of them take you by surprise, they will harm (or end) your ability to get hired.

Though you don't need to give the exact answers we give to the ten common questions listed in this chapter, they should get you started as you put together your responses for your phone interview, mock interview, and your interview at the company.

What is your greatest strength?

You should answer this question in an unabashed manner — that is, be very clear about what your biggest personal strength is. If you aren't sure, think about the one thing you're most passionate about.

What's more, talk about how you've used and demonstrated that strength. Talk about how you think that strength is rare, unique, and something that helps you stand apart from the crowd. Most important, tell the interviewers how you've used that strength to become a better software developer. It doesn't matter what your greatest strength is if it isn't valuable to your employer.

What is your greatest weakness?

This is a classic question designed to trap you. You have to avoid giving an answer that is actually a strength and pretend like it's a weakness as well as give an answer that's so transparently debilitating that your interviewers decide you shouldn't be hired.

For example, don't say that you're a perfectionist and so it's a weakness because you want everything to be perfect. Interviewers can see right through that kind of answer and it will make it appear as if you're trying to deceive the interviewers by not giving them honest answers.

On the other hand, if you say that you have mental issues and you're taking medication for it, then you've entered the TMI (too much information) zone and your interviewers will be persuaded that you shouldn't be hired. (Sadly, mental illness is still stigmatized in society.)

So, think of a real weakness that you've used to make yourself better. One example is to say that you're someone who always finds one more thing to fix and so in the past you had problems releasing products. Then you can follow up by saying how you've learned from that weakness by writing down what needs to be finished for the product to be released at the beginning of the project and how that approach made you a more effective software developer.

Where do you see yourself in five years?

This question is designed to disqualify you as a candidate. It's easy to respond to this question by saying, "I don't know." Though that's an honest answer, it's not a good one. You may be dismissed from the interview if you're even transparent about your intentions such as you're going to be working in a different job because you expect you'll hit a wall in your development within the next five years.

Instead, you need to answer the question by telling your interviewers that you're going to be growing professionally along with the company and tell them how you're going to do that. For example, you may tell them that you're going to improve not just your programming skills but also your mentoring skills. Then you can say you not only want to be the person on the team people come to for information or advice, but also you want to make the team the best it can be in the next five years so managers can be confident the team can produce any product for customers.

In sum, your answer needs to reflect that you know what you want your direction to be within the company — even if you say that you want to be the team manager, department manager, or part owner.

Why did you leave your last company?

Here's another question designed to disqualify you because you can answer it in the wrong way very easily. The best way to answer it is to always put a positive spin on your experience. A quick way to take yourself out of the running is to say you hated the job, you hated the boss, and/or you were fired.

If you can't say anything nice about your job or your boss, you can still give interviewers one or more good answers:

>> The job culture wasn't the right fit.

>> You recently moved to this area.

>> Your skill set wasn't being used fully and you felt that you didn't make the best contribution you could.

>> You're looking for new opportunities and challenges.

>> You wanted an opportunity to work with the technologies that the company you're interviewing with is using.

TIP

When you mention you want to work with new technologies, this is a good time to say how you've been learning these new technologies and applying them, such as in a side project or talking about them in your blog.

The moral of this story is to be honest in your answers but *don't* reveal anything negative.

Name a time you got into a conflict with a coworker, and how was that resolved?

This is another question to test your maturity or, to use the vernacular, get a sense of your emotional quotient (EQ). We've all had some kind of conflict with a coworker, no matter how small, because it's inevitable when you're working with different personalities in one location. Even if you've been working on your own for a while, you've probably had an issue with a customer either in person, on the phone, or in an email message.

No matter what conflict you think of from the past, you need to spin it in a positive light. Here's how:

>> Don't talk badly about your coworker or the person you were working with, such as a customer of your app who yelled at you.

>> Don't tell the interviewers that the other person was an idiot or that he or she made a mistake.

>> Tell the interviewers how you resolved the situation in a peaceful way.

>> Explain how you learned how to see the other person's point of view.

>> Discuss how you realized you were also wrong and how you grew from that realization.

>> Say how the experience helped teach you how to better manage conflict.

What the interviewer is looking for is how both you and the other person came to a resolution that was beneficial for the company overall.

What did you like about your last job?

When you prepare to answer this question, think about the things that will mirror the job you're applying for.

If you previously worked for a small company and you're applying to work at a big company, it won't make sense if you talk about how you liked the energy of working for that company. The interviewers will think that you're not going to be happy at the job you're applying for, so they'll wonder why you're applying for the job in the first place — and that if you're hired, you'll leave quickly.

Instead, talk about positive things in your last job that you enjoyed. Those things can include your boss and/or your coworkers who had personality traits and interests that you've noticed in some of the interviewers during your interview. You can talk about the work environment if your interviewers note their environment is much like the one you had at your last job. And based on your review of the job description, you can note that in your last job you used the same technology that you'll use in the job you're applying for, so you'll be a perfect fit.

What did you dislike?

This is another one of those "don't say anything negative" questions. Your interviewers want to see if you're a negative person when you have a chance to be, but don't take the bait.

Instead, you can say that there wasn't anything in particular that you really disliked about your last job — you were happy, you enjoyed working for the company, and you enjoyed your coworkers.

After you talk about the people and environment in your last job in glowing terms, make what you dislike seem like it's not a big deal. One explanation could be, "I just felt like my talents weren't being used to the fullest. I thought I could do a lot more for the company but there wasn't the opportunity."

This answer also doesn't include the word "challenge," which can be a red flag word for interviewers because they may get the impression that if you're not challenged enough in your job, then you'll leave sooner rather than later.

Why do you want to work for us (or this company)?

Answering this question is a good opportunity for you to show that you researched the company before you came in for the interview. Depending on your company research, here's how you can respond:

>> Talk about the history and culture of the company, such as, "I really like the founder's mission and how he started out working in his garage just like I did. I aspire to fulfill that mission."

> » Tell the interviewers how you can make an impact and how your skill set perfectly matches what the company is looking for.
>
> » Explain how you're excited to raise the bar on the team to the next level and how you can help the programming team do that.

REMEMBER

Your answers need to show that you really know both the job and the company, and that you're not just someone who would take any job — you will only interview for and work for a company that has high standards. That will tell your interviewers that you have high standards, too, and will help persuade your interviewers that you're not only worth hiring, but you'll contribute to the high standards set by the company.

Why should we hire you?

You need to frame your answer to this question in terms of what's valuable to them. Don't talk about why you want the job or how it benefits you. Instead, talk about the benefits you'll give the company after they hire you.

This is the time to brag about yourself a little bit — that you're the best candidate for the job because you're really skilled at the programming language or technology, talk about your accomplishments, and talk about how you continually show leadership in the software development community through your online resources. This can also be the time that you take your self-published book out of your briefcase to show off.

TIP

Before you start to annoy your interviewers with all your swagger, switch gears and tell about how you can make the team better. That is, you're the kind of person who figures out what needs to be done, figures out how to do it, and gets it done. You should note that you're a low-maintenance employee, but you're not just someone who will go off in a corner and work on a job — you're also great at working with teams to get the job done and spread the credit around.

Why are you the best candidate for this job?

Interviewers will ask this question right after why they should hire you, and this is not a time to be humble. If you're humble (or, worse, self-deprecating) then you're blowing the chance to describe all your best qualities.

So, follow up on your previous answers about why you should be hired by showing and giving an overview of what you're doing:

>> You have a blog that you update regularly.

>> You have a YouTube channel that not only contains a number of instructional videos but also your video résumé and vlogs — and you add more content regularly.

>> You post new audio podcasts frequently.

>> You're written at least one self-published book.

>> You're commenting and answering questions from fellow programmers on software development websites, including GitHub and Stack Overflow.

>> You've spoken at local developer, business events, and/or large developer conferences.

>> You attend developer conferences as often as your schedule allows so you can continue to make new connections and learn about the latest trends. Then you pass along what you learned from those conferences to your readers and viewers.

If you've done most — if not all — of these things and continue to work on many of them (such as writing blog posts and producing videos), then you're going to command the interview room. Now you can use that position to show interviewers how you've applied your expertise in past jobs:

>> Tell how you've helped other companies in the past that you worked for.

>> Show that people who work with you now and/or have worked with you in the past have written recommendations endorsing you.

>> Explain how you communicate your points effectively.

>> Discuss how you've made projects successful.

>> Describe you're a good team player and enhance the performance of the entire team.

>> Talk about your leadership qualities and how you've influenced people.

You may think of other qualities that you want to tell the interviewers, but you get the idea: This is your opportunity for you to shine and leave stars in your interviewers' eyes — and you only have a short amount of time to do it. Make every second count.

Chapter **17**

Ten Reasons Your Résumé Will End up in the Round File

Your résumé will be the first or second thing (after your cover letter) company representatives tasked with hiring a new programmer will read to learn more about you. A résumé serves as a concise summary of your accomplishments and the only impression prospective employers will have about your abilities until they talk to you in an interview.

The initial reviewer of résumés acts as the company gatekeeper, and that person will determine if you're worth considering for the job.

What's more, your résumé will be put in the shredder if you give a poor performance during one or more of your interviews. You can't come across as anything other than polite and straightforward if you want the job.

So, it's important that you don't make even one of the ten errors we discuss in this chapter. Feel free to use this chapter as a checklist as you review your résumé and prepare for your interview.

Your Résumé Has Typos, Spelling Errors, and Uses Incorrect Grammar

The first and most obvious problem a reviewer will find in your résumé is a typo, a spelling error, or incorrect grammar. It's very easy to make these mistakes, which is one good reason why we recommend using a résumé writing service in Chapter 5.

So what, you say? Just a little typo here or spelling error there isn't a big deal because we all make mistakes, right?

An employer is judging you from the moment the person reviewing your résumé and cover letter takes a look at both. Just one error means you're not just unprofessional, but you also lack attention to detail.

REMEMBER

In software development, attention to detail means the difference between getting an application completed on time, getting good reviews from customers, and/or getting the next round of funding from investors so the company can stay afloat and employees can keep their jobs.

Your Résumé Is Too Long

It's tempting to tell the company everything about your employment history in your résumé, especially if you've had a long career, because you want to impress the reader with how much experience you have and how many programming languages you know.

Resist that temptation and put yourself in the shoes of the résumé reviewer. Reviewers have dozens if not hundreds of résumés to go through, and it becomes overwhelming not only to read through your pages of experience but also to pick out what experiences you have that are relevant to the job opening. We bet you dollars to donuts that you'll agree it's easier and faster to put a long résumé in the "to shred" pile.

So, you need to tailor a different résumé for each job opening. Start with the master copy of your résumé, create a copy for the company, and then edit that copy so that it fits the job description and is to the point. A one-page résumé is ideal, but don't make it longer than two pages.

REMEMBER

You want to tell your prospective employer that you're valuable to the company because your skills fit the job description to a T. A short résumé will not only tell your prospective employer that, but also potential interviewers may be curious to learn more — especially if you add links to your online resources such as your blog and social media profiles.

You Start Your Résumé with an Objective

A company is not interested about what you're looking for or what your career objectives are. Putting an objective at the beginning of your résumé shows that you're only interested in what value you can get from the company, not what value you can give it.

What's more, having objectives in your résumé shows that you wrote it because no professional résumé service will put objectives in a résumé, that you had no one who knows about writing modern résumés review yours, and that you never read Chapter 5 in this book.

Your Résumé Layout Looks Sloppy and Is Hard to Read

The presentation of your résumé determines if it'll be read by anyone other than the initial reviewer. Now you may think that because you're a computer programmer, your presentation doesn't matter — it's the code examples that count!

Remember when we said that the initial reviewer is the gatekeeper? That person is also an expert in one thing, and it's not computer programming. So, you need to win over the perception of that gatekeeper and ensure the résumé is designed so that it's easy to read and presents your information in a way that reviewers can find what they need. A professional résumé service will ensure that your résumé is well-designed.

TIP

If you've decided not to take our advice and you write and design your résumé yourself, here's an even better idea (because we're always thinking): Ask one or all of your mock interviewers to review your résumé before you send them out. Having those mock interviewers pick apart your résumé may not feel good, but doing so will give you a far better chance of having a résumé that glows when the reviewer reads it. (We're not Joe Namath, so we can't guarantee it.)

You Have Inappropriate Material on Social Media

You may have links to your social media profiles in your résumé, but even if you don't, the initial reviewer will likely search for your profiles online. If the reviewer doesn't but sends your résumé to others for further review, those reviewers will definitely search for your name on Google, within social media websites, or (probably) both.

If company reviewers find anything that they think is questionable if not downright objectionable, they'll run, not walk, to the shredder to rid themselves of your résumé. (You likely won't hear anything back from the company about the job, either.)

We give you guidance for cleaning up your social media profiles and presenting a professional image in Chapter 5. We won't mind if you bookmark this page and read that chapter so you can clean up your profiles first before you continue reading this chapter.

You Lie during the Phone Screen or Interview

Employment, like any other relationship, is based on trust. Your employer reasonably expects that you'll get your work done, do a good job, and be honest. However, if you lie during an interview because you think it's better to give an answer, you'd be embarrassed if you didn't, and/or you think not answering will cost you the job, the opposite is true.

Presume your interviewers are experienced at interviewing and will know when you're lying either because at least one of them knows the subject matter and will call you out on your lie immediately, they'll see your mannerisms change, or (likely) both. When that happens, expect to be thanked for your time and escorted out of the building.

If you don't know the answer to a question, say so and put a positive spin on it. If you honestly haven't studied the specific issue the interviewer asked you about, you can say, "You know, I haven't encountered that yet, but I will now because I'm curious."

Or, if you don't remember the answer to the question, you could say, "You know what? I should probably know the answer but I don't remember what it is. Could you please tell me? Because I'm really curious to know about it so I can study that more."

When you answer confidently and in a way that tells your interviewers that you want to learn, they'll more likely think your lack of an answer isn't a big deal and they'll move on to the next question.

WARNING

It seems acceptable, especially if you take your behavioral cues from politics, that you should "double down" if someone says you're lying. That is, you should be argumentative and insist that you're telling the truth when at least one interviewer says you aren't. This strategy only compounds your problem — because being argumentative during your interview isn't professional — and will reinforce the interviewers' perceptions that they shouldn't hire you.

You Are Arrogant and/or Argumentative

An interview can feel contentious or even threatening. You may think that you'll have to defend yourself — aggressively, if necessary — because you don't want to look weak. In reality, that strategy will expose a couple of your big weaknesses: You're immature and you can't get along with other people.

When you've gone through at least one mock interview so you've worked out any and all of your behavioral issues, and you know you're a good programmer, it'll be very difficult for an interview to fluster you.

Instead, you'll know that if an interviewer asks you a question that you don't know the answer to, or challenges the answer to your question, you don't need to argue. You also don't need to put up defenses and become arrogant such as by saying the interviewer doesn't know what he's talking about.

You can simply remain calm, focus on the question or answer instead of the questioner, and discuss the issue. If you can't, then you've just told the interviewers that you're not confident in your abilities. Don't be surprised if the head interviewer ends the interview right there.

REMEMBER

If you were calm and collected during your mock interview, don't change your behavior because you're in a real interview. It's human to want to change your behavior when you find yourself in a different situation, such as when you get promoted. Instead, in your real interview, double down on showing the confidence you displayed in your mock interview.

You Have a Bad Reputation

The world is smaller than you think, especially if you're looking for work in one city or region. Always presume that employees at various employers talk to each other because there are plenty of opportunities to do so, such as at conferences, business luncheons, and Meetup events for human resources people, developers, and other groups.

If you developed a bad reputation at one company where you've had social issues with other employees, had issues with your boss, and have burned bridges, that behavior will catch up to you when you're looking for another job.

What's a good sign that you have a bad reputation? When you send out at least 10 to 20 résumés and cover letters and you either receive generic rejection letters or no response at all from every single company you've applied to.

Getting the feeling that you've created a bad reputation is an experience that you'll always remember, but if and when you make a commitment to change and build a good reputation instead, do things to make yourself stand out as we discuss how to do in Chapter 15. Today is a great day to start.

TIP

Professional résumé services may have their fingers on the pulse of the technology community and make a list of who has a bad reputation so they can prepare for that if a person on the list wants to use their service. A professional résumé service may offer services to rebuild your reputation — for an extra fee. So, having a bad reputation may also require you to shell out money you didn't expect to spend to get your foot in an employer's door.

You Don't Dress Properly for the Interview

People discriminate naturally, so when you arrive at the company for your interview, the first thing your interviewers and other company personnel will notice is how you're dressed. And if you're not dressed professionally and groomed properly, no matter if a company representative says you can dress casually, then you're telling the interviewers that you're not professional.

When interviewers see that you've taken the time and effort to dress properly and look like a professional, they'll not only see you as a professional but also as someone who is an excellent programmer — just as you said in your cover letter and résumé.

One or more interviewers may comment on the way you look and say that you don't have to dress that way in the job. That's a good sign that you've made a positive impression, because some of your interviewers think you're worthy of being hired.

You Give the Impression You're Hiding Something

If you go into an interview, it's natural to feel somewhat nervous if you haven't practiced before — and especially if you haven't interviewed for a job before or for a long while. That's why we recommend holding at least one mock interview so you can get the butterflies out of your system.

Building up your confidence during a mock interview has another beneficial side effect — you'll avoid giving the company interviewers any one of the following several negative impressions:

>> You're hiding something — maybe you lied on your résumé.

>> You don't do well in high pressure situations.

>> You're not an authentic person.

When you're nervous, you'll make at least one interviewer nervous and you may not "click" with those people. When you're confident, you'll create a connection between you and your interviewers, and it's more likely you'll come across as someone who can be trusted, who knows what you're doing, and that you're a genuine person.

REMEMBER

There may be one or more interviewers you won't connect with regardless because they have some issues, such as they may be intimidated by your skill set or another programmer might dilute their power. If you need to learn how to deal with different interviewer personalities, go read Chapter 8.

Chapter **18**

Ten Useful Websites to Check Out

There are plenty of great websites for information not just about how to solve a wide variety of programming puzzles but also about how to find jobs and even get your résumé and cover letter written by certified professionals.

It was hard for us to select only ten websites to recommend to you, but we think these ten sites will give you the tools and information you need to succeed. We write about some of these sources in more detail in earlier chapters in the book, but if you haven't read those chapters yet, here's your chance to learn about them.

LeetCode

The LeetCode website (https://leetcode.com) is one of the best places on the web to find and practice programming problems. All you have to do to view the list of questions is click the View Questions link on the home page to open the Questions page shown in Figure 18-1.

What's more, you'll find problems to practice that are asked of interviewees at various large companies, including Facebook, Google, LinkedIn, Amazon, and many others. Just click one of the companies listed in the Companies section on the right side of the Questions page.

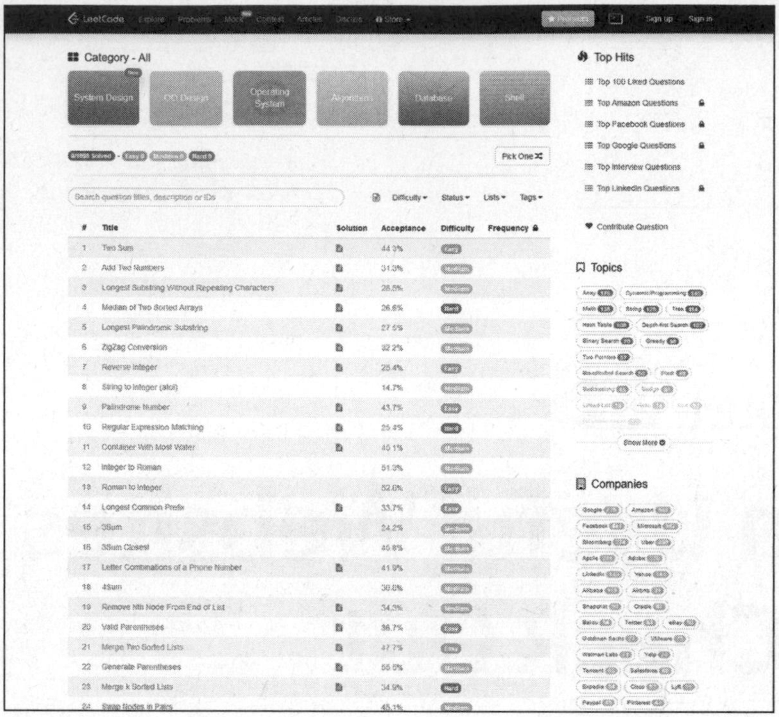

FIGURE 18-1: The LeetCode Questions page shows a list of programming problems in all categories.

Source: `https://leetcode.com`

If you want to get the most out of the LeetCode site, sign up for a membership. LeetCode gives you the option of signing up for a monthly plan if you only want to use it while you're looking for a job, or for a yearly plan if you want to use LeetCode as a resource for one calendar year. As of this writing, the monthly subscription costs $35 per month and the yearly subscription costs $159 per year.

Interview Cake

The Interview Cake website (`www.interviewcake.com`) teaches you how to prepare for and succeed in a programming interview. If you need free information right away, the website offers a seven-day email course; just enter your email address on the home page. What's more, you can get free information by clicking the Interview Tips link in the blue menu bar at the top of the home page shown in Figure 18-2.

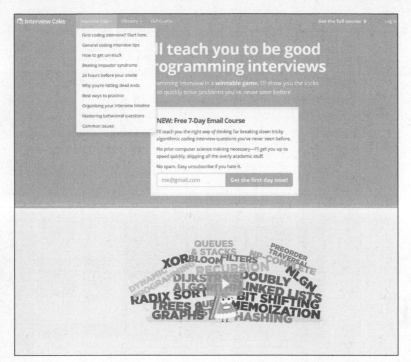

Source: www.interviewcake.com

Click one of the topics in the drop-down menu to get more information about the topic. If you want to preview Interview Cake's full course, click Full Course to the right of the Interview Tips and Glossary menu options. The free preview lets you look at sample questions in a wide variety of areas, and the bottom of the page contains links to programming problems posed by different companies.

If you're sold and want to purchase a course, Interview Cake offers two: a "crunch time" course that allows three weeks of access to site information for $149, and the full course for $249 that gives you one year of full access to the site. (Though the site also offers a $4,900 course with one-on-one coaching, as of this writing this option was sold out.) If you're a student, you may qualify for discounted pricing. And both courses come with a money-back guarantee.

Reddit Programming Forum

Reddit is one of the largest community forum sites on the web, so you probably won't be surprised that Reddit has one of the biggest online programmer communities, too. Just go to www.reddit.com/r/programming to view the latest conversations as shown in Figure 18-3.

FIGURE 18-3:
Posts on Reddit are listed in reverse chronological order with the most recent post at the top of the list.

Source: www.reddit.com

Scroll up and down the page to view the list of the most popular posts. Each post includes the subject title so you can click the link and view the entire post as well as comments left about that post.

If you want to comment about any post or write a post yourself, you have to sign up for a Reddit account by clicking the Join button within the Community Details section to the right of the posts list. This site does come with paid advertisements within the feeds, as you can see in Figure 18-3, but that's the price you have to pay instead of real money.

Before you post, be sure to read the programming rules and information within the Info section on the right side of the posts list. Read frequently asked questions by clicking the FAQ link just above the top of the posts list.

Simple Programmer

This popular programming blog (https://simpleprogrammer.com) is dedicated to teaching software developers soft skills and career skills (see Figure 18-4).

FIGURE 18-4: The Articles tab is opened automatically so you can read the latest Simple Programmer blog articles.

This website includes articles written by various programmers. To read an entire article, click the article graphic or the name of the article. If you want to write for Simple Programmer, move the mouse pointer over About in the menu bar and then click Write for Us in the drop-down menu.

The menu bar also includes options for you to purchase various products and get free courses and resources, including career tools, programmer gifts, and more. When you click the About menu option, the person who created and maintains the site may be very familiar.

Pluralsight Design Patterns Library

If you want to learn design patterns backwards and forwards so you can use them in your daily development life, the Pluralsight website has a detailed library of design patterns at `www.pluralsight.com/courses/patterns-library` (see Figure 18-5).

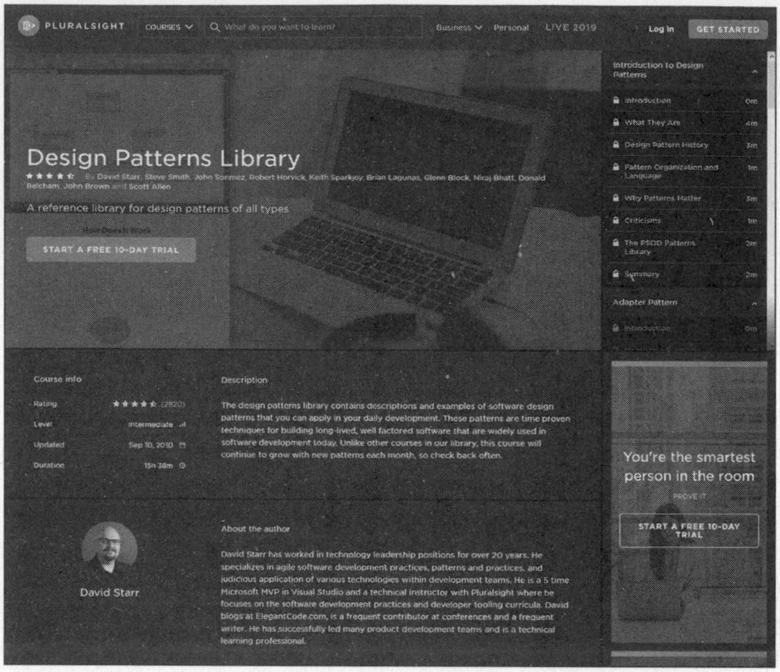

FIGURE 18-5: Information about design patterns appears on the right side of the Pluralsight web page.

Source: www.pluralsight.com

You can sign up for a 10-day free trial to view all the components in the library and see if it's worth it for you. One enticement is that the library adds new patterns every month.

After the 10-day free trial is over, you need to sign up for a Pluralsight membership, which includes access to the entire Pluralsight library. As of this writing, Pluralsight offers three different membership plans:

- A monthly plan for $35.
- An annual plan for $299.
- A premium annual plan for $499 that includes certification practice exams, interactive courses, and the ability to build projects.

Pluralsight also offers memberships for business teams starting at $579 per user per year and enterprises starting at $779 per user per year.

Hired.com

If you live in certain metropolitan areas in the United States, Canada, and Europe, then you may be interested in joining Hired.com (www.hired.com), shown in Figure 18-6. This site allows you to create an account for free and have companies apply to interview you for a job.

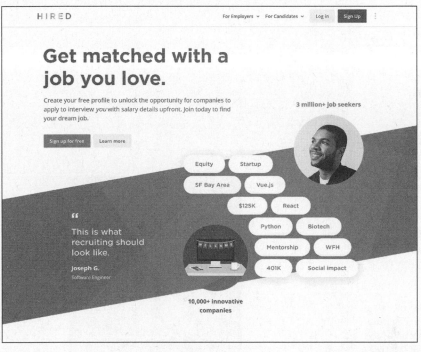

FIGURE 18-6: Sign up for Hired. com by clicking the Sign Up for Free button on the home page.

As you scroll down the home page, you'll see the metropolitan areas Hired.com serves, the types of roles and specialties Hired.com supports (including software developers), and a sample of how many different companies are looking for candidates on Hired.com.

After you sign up, you need to create a profile much as you would create a résumé, but your Hired.com profile can also include photos of your favorite projects and links to your personal work. Hired.com also promises that your profile will be hidden to your current employer and past employers.

142 Resources for Mastering the Coding Interview

The BetterProgramming blog hosted by the Medium blogging platform has an article that contains links to 142 coding interview resources. After you access the website at `https://medium.com/better-programming/the-software-engineering-study-guide-bac25b8b61eb` (see Figure 18-7), scroll down the page to see the entire list of resource links.

FIGURE 18-7:
We promise the resource links appear once you scroll down the page past the large cover photo.

Source: https://medium.com

Links are categorized in a variety of topics starting with a list of five classic coding problems and ending with a list of design patterns. Some categories include videos that tell you how to answer questions such as an Amazon coding interview question. Most links tell you what opens when you click the link, such as a blog post or a video.

And yes, we did count and confirm that there are indeed 142 links — as well as the five bonus classic coding problems at the beginning of the article — for you to view at your leisure.

Stack Overflow Careers

The Stack Overflow website is a popular community site for programmers, but you may not know that it's also a place where companies post jobs and search for the right programmers they need.

View the list of job postings by clicking the Find a Job button on the Stack Overflow home page or go to `https://stackoverflow.com/jobs` to open the Jobs page shown in Figure 18-8.

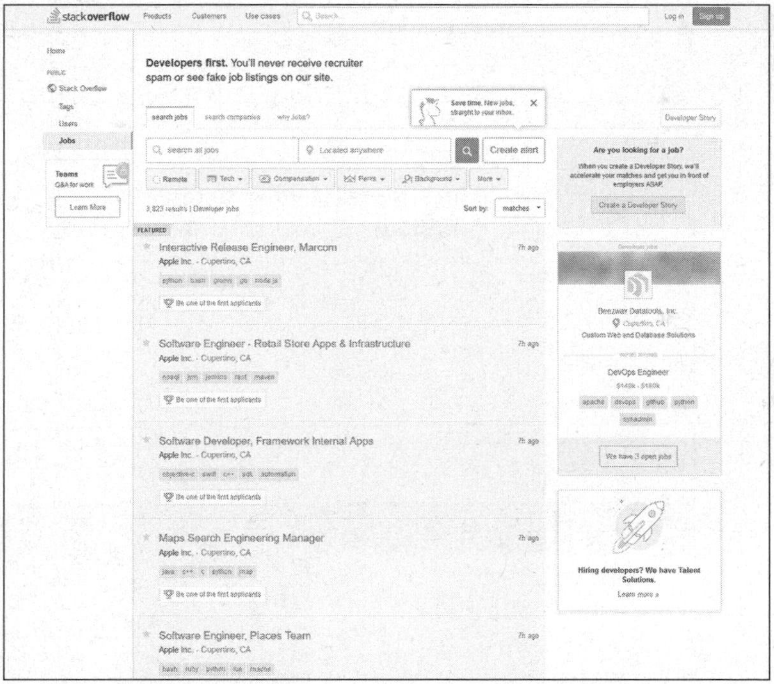

FIGURE 18-8: A list of the most recent job postings appears in reverse chronological order with the most recent job listed first.

Source: *https://stackoverflow.com*

Above the list you can search for the job title you want by typing your search terms in the Search All Jobs box, and then click the Located Anywhere box to find the location where you want to find a job. When you're finished, click the blue magnifying glass button and you'll see a list of all jobs that meet your criteria.

If you're looking for a job and want employers to find you, Stack Overflow invites you to click on the Create a Developer Story button to the right of the list. A "developer story" is an online résumé so employers who are looking for you can find you more easily. However, you have to sign up for a free Stack Overflow account to create that story.

So, sign up, set up your developer story, and let Stack Overflow make it easier for you to find the job you deserve. Slicker than a box of rocks.

Interviewing.io

If you're nervous about the prospect of an interview, especially at a large technology company, check out the interviewing.io website (`https://interviewing.io`) shown in Figure 18-9. This site allows you to schedule free (yes, free) interviews with senior software engineers who will give you valuable feedback and tips for acing your real interview.

FIGURE 18-9:
Sign up for a free membership by clicking the Give It a Try button on the home page.

Source: `https://interviewing.io`

Your free membership unlocks the ability to hold a mock online interview with questions about algorithmic problems, system design problems, and more from an engineer at one of a variety of large companies including:

» Google

» Facebook

» Microsoft

» Amazon

» Dropbox

You choose the company you want to interview with and you're anonymous throughout the mock interview. If you're not sure about joining interviewing.io and/or want to see what an online interview looks like, you can scroll down the home page and click the Watch Some Recordings of Past Interviews link and see what happens in mock interviews.

If you do well in the mock interview, you can "unmask" yourself so the interviewer can see who you are and you can set up an onsite, real interview with that company quickly. Slicker than a box of rocks.

Information Technology Résumé Services

Jennifer Hay is not only an excellent résumé writer — she was the first certified résumé writer in the United States — she's also certified in career guidance, business intelligence, and information technology.

Hay's business, Information Technology Résumé Services (ITRS), is a great résumé writing service that services the United States, not just the Seattle area where ITRS is headquartered. Go to `www.itresumeservice.com`, shown in Figure 18-10, to learn more.

ITRS provides résumé writing services for a variety of IT professionals, including data specialists, IT administrators, and software developers. What's more, ITRS provides free tips and articles as well as several low-cost and no-cost training videos.

Source: www.itresumeservice.com

FIGURE 18-10:
You can read sample résumés by clicking Read More within the Résumé Samples section on the home page.

Even if you think you'll have your résumé and cover letter produced by a local or regional company, why not compare what Hay has done for her clients with the sample résumés that other companies provide? It never hurts to compare other companies' work with samples from one of the best résumé and cover letter writing companies around.

Chapter **19**

Ten Great Books to Read

There are plenty of great books for information not just about preparing for your in-person interview, but also about how to solve a wide variety of programming puzzles. We have ten books we think you should consider reading alongside this one.

It was hard for us to select only ten books to recommend to you, but we think they will give you the tools and information you need to succeed. We write about some of these sources in more detail in earlier chapters in the book, but if you haven't read those chapters yet, here's your chance to learn about them.

Cracking the Coding Interview

Gayle Laakmann McDowell, owner of CareerCup in the San Francisco Bay Area, has published six editions of her best-selling book, *Cracking the Coding Interview*. This book contains 189 programming questions, including many algorithm-style problems, and their solutions.

The book also has a lot of good advice about how to prepare for and ace a programming interview, which isn't surprising because CareerCup offers personal interview preparation services. Though the sixth edition was published in July 2015, the book is still current and as of this writing remains a number one bestseller in the computer programming languages category on Amazon.

What's more, the CareerCup website (www.careercup.com) has a list of recent interview questions that readers have submitted so you can see what companies are asking programming candidates. The site also includes videos of mock interviews conducted by McDowell with unscripted candidate reactions to learn from.

Never Split the Difference

Though we're negotiators from the time we're very young, negotiating your benefits package at your potential new employer can seem overwhelming. After all, your life and your ability to live the way you want are on the line.

So, don't start negotiating until you've read *Never Split the Difference: Negotiating as if Your Life Depended on It.* The book was written by Chris Voss, a former FBI lead international kidnapping negotiator, and award-winning business author Tahl Raz. (The book also has a five-star customer rating on Amazon.)

Saving lives honed Voss's negotiation abilities, and he shares nine negotiation principles that may seem counterintuitive, but will give you the competitive edge — from establishing a rapport with the people you're negotiating with to how to bargain so you get the price (or, in this case, the salary and benefits) you want.

Programming Pearls

If you're looking for a book that will tell you how to solve algorithm problems in C and C++, then the classic *Programming Pearls* by Jon Bentley is the book you need. This book was originally written in 1986 and updated in a second edition in 1999, and despite the book's age, the concepts and problems contained within are those you need to know to prepare yourself to answer interview questions.

Chapters in this book follow the same pattern:

>> Choosing the process of finding the right algorithm to quickly find a solution that's effective and accurate.

>> Code profiling to get the correct answer to a problem.

> » Programming principles for you to remember.

> » A final list of problems for you to solve.

When you finish reading this book and solve the problems within it, you'll be a better programmer and ready to pass any interview with flying colors.

Daily Coding Problem

This book by Lawrence Wu and Alex Miller has the subtitle, *Get Exceptionally Good at Coding Interviews by Solving One Problem Every Day.*

Wu and Miller are both software engineers. Miller has interviewed hundreds of candidates for companies such as Yelp and Pinterest, and each question is based on an actual interview question asked by large tech companies. You'll answer questions in a variety of categories including:

> » Arrays

> » Strings

> » Sorting

> » Recursion

> » Linked lists

> » Hash tables

> » Stacks and queues

> » Randomized algorithms

These categories are just a sample of all the categories in the book, and you can decide which questions you want to work on based on the job you're interviewing for. After you get into a groove and solve your daily programming problem, you'll feel confident that you can answer any question by the time you reach the last page of the book.

The Complete Software Developer's Career Guide

This book is written by someone you may find familiar (one of the coauthors of this book), and is for every programmer no matter his or her skill level. It asks (and answers) several important questions including:

» What programming language should I master first?

» How do I fill the gaps in my programming knowledge?

» How do I get around the "chicken and egg" problems of companies requiring three to five years of job experience that I don't have?

» Is getting a computer science degree a necessity or a waste of time?

» How do I find a great coding bootcamp so I'm not scammed out of a lot of money?

» Should I take contract work or hold out for a salaried position, and which option brings me more money?

» How do I manage my boss so that he doesn't micromanage me, but so that I can still help him succeed?

This book discusses the human side of software development and when you finish reading it, you'll understand why Amazon lists the book as a top seller in job interviewing.

The Imposter's Handbook

This ebook written by Rob Conery is only available on the Big Machine website (https://bigmachine.io/products/the-imposters-handbook) shown in Figure 19-1.

Conery bills the book as one for people who want to teach themselves computer programming without having to go through formal schooling. Conery did this by diving into all the topics that a typical computer science degree requires from the Stanford University website. Then he wrote a book that covered all those topics, including design principles, algorithms, design patterns, and data structures.

FIGURE 19-1:
A slideshow
of pages appears
on the Big
Machine home
page so you can
preview the book.

What's more, Conery offers a print edition of the book for $49.99 (as of this writing; the ebook version costs $30), which includes 17 video walkthroughs so you have a full understanding of what Conery covers in the book.

If you like the book, Conery invites you to purchase the second volume, *The Imposter's Handbook Season 2*, which also costs $30, so you can learn about advanced topics, including information theory and blockchain. You can also buy both volumes for only $49 instead of the normal $59.

How to Win Friends and Influence People

The Dale Carnegie book, *How to Win Friends and Influence People* is considered the seminal book for learning how to improve their interpersonal skills so people can get the outcome they want from any situation. Carnegie died in 1955, but his book has been updated constantly since then, with the last edition published in 1998.

This book teaches you

>> six ways to make people like you (smiling is involved),

>> twelve ways to get people to adopt your way of thinking, and

>> nine ways to change people without making them angry or resentful.

After multiple editions published and over 15 million copies sold, the book is still relevant today and will be relevant as long as humans behave the way they do.

Programming Interviews Exposed

John Mongan, Noah Kindler, and Eric Giguere wrote the fourth edition of this book, subtitled *Coding Your Way Through the Interview*. Because this book is published by Wrox, a sister Wiley book brand, it's the natural complement to this book.

Programming Interviews Exposed goes further than this book by primarily covering programming problems you'll encounter in the phone screen as well as in the actual interview, including:

>> Arrays and strings

>> Concurrency

>> Counting, measuring, and ordering puzzles

>> Data science, random numbers, and statistics problems

>> Databases

>> Design patterns

>> Graphical and special puzzles

>> Graphics and bit manipulation

>> Knowledge-based questions

>> Linked lists

>> Object-oriented programming

>> Recursion

>> Recursion, string, and duplicate questions during a phone screen

- » Sorting

- » The best way to analyze your solution, especially by using the Big O analysis

- » Trees and graphs

When you pick up our book, pick up *Programming Interviews Exposed* as well so you can get a full understanding of the programming interview process. Our book takes you through the basics and the human element, and *Programming Interviews Exposed* uses a soup-to-nuts approach to tell you about all the programming questions (and answers) you should know.

The Passionate Programmer

This book by Chad Fowler talks about approaching programming holistically. That is, not looking at the next job but at your career as a whole so you can drive your career in the direction you want. Though the book was published in 2009, the concepts in the book are as fresh today as they were then.

Through a series of essays in the book, Fowler shows you what your career looks like from a 30,000 feet review so you can see what you need to do now as well as 5, 10, and 20 years from now. That work includes creating a structured plan for keeping your skills fresh and your brain thinking.

When you're thinking ahead, you can see what skills are becoming important and in what fields. You also learn to assess your skills and how to train yourself to be marketable to companies that use those new technologies. You'll find yourself working on more interesting technologies and getting paid more in the process.

In sum, if you're looking to become a leader in the software development world, you should buy this book, which is available only as an ebook on Amazon Kindle.

Head First Design Patterns

This book by Eric Freeman, Bert Bates, Kathy Sierra, and Elisabeth Robson was published in 2004 — which you can tell from the model on the cover who looks like rock singer Gwen Stefani in those days — but the information is still relevant because many design patterns haven't changed over the years.

The subtitle of this book is *A Brain-Friendly Guide,* and the book lives up to that claim by providing not only simple explanations of common design patterns, but also many visual examples to reinforce the concepts explained in the text.

The book covers an extensive list of patterns you may encounter during your programming career, including:

>> Adapter and façade

>> Command

>> Compound

>> Decorator

>> Factory

>> Iterator and composite

>> Observer

>> Proxy

>> Singleton

>> State

>> Template Method

The book ends with a chapter about how to apply these patterns in the real world and an appendix of other patterns that aren't as important to know but you may encounter in your work.

If you're the type of person who needs simplified information and illustrations that help reinforce concepts, this book will make it easier for you to understand design pattern concepts, why they're important, how to recognize different design patterns, and how to use them in your code.

Index

Numerics

proxy, 131
recursion
  defined, 131
  direct, 131–132
  indirect, 132
  online resources, 134
  recursion algorithms, 133
  recursion word problem example, 134
  stack overflow and, 133
  singleton, 130
Design Patterns (Gamma, Helm, Johnson, and
    Vlissides), 128
Desire step, AIDA model of cover letter, 71–72
direct recursion, 131–132
DiSC Behavior Inventory, 91
double-linked lists, 119
dressing professionally, 17–18, 216–217

E

Emerson, Ralph Waldo, 173
employment gaps,explaining, 82
enqueueing message, 122
event speaking, 199–201
Everything Store, The (Stone), 24
extracurricular activities, 77–78

F

façade design pattern, 130–131
Facebook. *See also* social media
  cleaning up online image, 61–62
  programming forums, 110
face-to-face meetings
  in-person interviews
    communicating value, 18
    dressing professionally, 17–18
    preparing for, 17
  networking events, 12–13
  programming events, 111
factory design pattern, 130
feedback, requesting
  mock interviews, 114
  post-interview, 115, 170

First In, First Out (FIFO), queues, 122
flexibility, importance of, 84–85
following up, post-interview, 168–169
401(k) retirement plan, 174
Fowler, Chad, 237
Free2X Webcam Recorder, 37
Freeman, Eric, 237

G

GeeksforGeeks website, 143–144
Giguere, Eric, 153, 236
GitHub
  establishing profile, 192–193
  finding unadvertised jobs via, 52
  rebranding with, 59
Glassdoor website, 179–180
Google
  advancement opportunities in, 167
  company culture, 46
  ranking on Comparably site, 180–181
  style of interviewing, 22
Google searches
  asking friends to search for you, 58
  finding professional résumé service, 65
  glassdoor competitors, 178–179
  by interviewers, 25
  keywords, 196
  practice interview questions, 93
  recursive program examples, 134
  revealing past problems or criminal activity, 60
  sorting algorithms animation, 144
  of yourself to examine online image,
    56–58
Google Sites, 36

H

HackerEarth website, 145–146
hashes
  collision, 120
  defined, 120–121
  hash maps, 121
Hay, Jennifer, 229–230

About the Authors

Eric Butow is the owner of Butow Communications Group (BCG) in Jackson, California. BCG offers website design, online marketing, and technical documentation services for businesses. He has written 32 computing and user experience books. His most recent books include *Samsung Gear S2 For Dummies*, *Pro iOS Security and Forensics*, and *Instagram For Dummies*.

When he's not working in (and on) his business or writing books, you can find Eric enjoying time with his friends, walking around the historic Gold Rush town of Jackson, and helping his mother manage her infant and toddler daycare business.

John Sonmez is a software developer and the author of two best-selling books, *The Complete Software Developer's Career Guide* and *Soft Skills: The Software Developer's Life Manual*. He's also the founder of the Simple Programmer blog and YouTube channel, where he reaches 1.4 million software developers yearly with a central message: Technical skills alone aren't enough for a successful career — or life.

John also is the founder and owner of Bulldog Mindset, where he teaches men to build mental toughness, financial independence, physical fitness, and how to improve their dating lives.

He's also a real estate investor and marathoner, and you can find him running around the beaches of sunny San Diego.

Dedications

To everyone who never stopped believing in me. —Eric Butow

To your future self, the one that's buried deep and waiting to get out.
—John Sonmez

Authors' Acknowledgments

I'd like to thank my co-author, John Sonmez, who's a great guy to work with. My thanks as well to my literary agent Matt Wagner at Fresh Books, Inc. I also want to thank all the pros at Wiley who made this book possible, especially acquisitions editor Katie Mohr and project editor Katharine Dvorak. And I thank you for buying this book. —Eric Butow

I'd like to thank my co-author, Eric Butow, who put up with my crazy schedule and kept the book on track. I'd also like to thank everyone at Wiley who did the hard work of wrangling two authors to write a book and making it great. —John Sonmez

Publisher's Acknowledgments

Associate Publisher: Katie Mohr

Project Editor: Katharine Dvorak

Proofreader: Debbye Butler

Editorial Assistant: Matthew Lowe

Production Editor: Mohammed Zafar Ali

Cover Image: © PeopleImages/iStock.com

Leverage the power

Dummies is the global leader in the reference category and one of the most trusted and highly regarded brands in the world. No longer just focused on books, customers now have access to the dummies content they need in the format they want. Together we'll craft a solution that engages your customers, stands out from the competition, and helps you meet your goals.

Advertising & Sponsorships

Connect with an engaged audience on a powerful multimedia site, and position your message alongside expert how-to content. Dummies.com is a one-stop shop for free, online information and know-how curated by a team of experts.

- Targeted ads
- Video
- Email Marketing
- Microsites
- Sweepstakes sponsorship

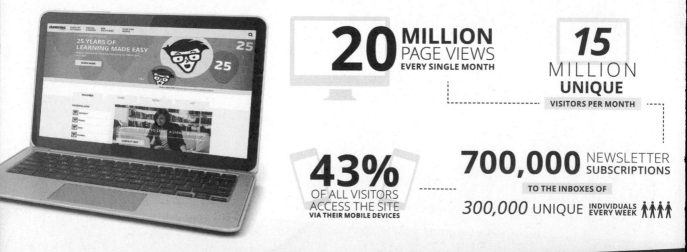

20 MILLION PAGE VIEWS EVERY SINGLE MONTH

15 MILLION UNIQUE VISITORS PER MONTH

43% OF ALL VISITORS ACCESS THE SITE VIA THEIR MOBILE DEVICES

700,000 NEWSLETTER SUBSCRIPTIONS TO THE INBOXES OF

300,000 UNIQUE INDIVIDUALS EVERY WEEK

# of dummies

Custom Publishing

Reach a global audience in any language by creating a solution that will differentiate you from competitors, amplify your message, and encourage customers to make a buying decision.

- Apps
- Books
- eBooks
- Video
- Audio
- Webinars

Brand Licensing & Content

Leverage the strength of the world's most popular reference brand to reach new audiences and channels of distribution.

For more information, visit dummies.com/biz

PERSONAL ENRICHMENT

Staying Sharp dummies	**Facebook** dummies	**Guitar** dummies	**Investing** dummies	**Beekeeping** dummies	**Digital Photography** dummies
9781119187790 USA $26.00 CAN $31.99 UK £19.99	9781119179030 USA $21.99 CAN $25.99 UK £16.99	9781119293354 USA $24.99 CAN $29.99 UK £17.99	9781119293347 USA $22.99 CAN $27.99 UK £16.99	9781119310068 USA $22.99 CAN $27.99 UK £16.99	9781119235606 USA $24.99 CAN $29.99 UK £17.99
Meditation dummies	**Pregnancy** ALL-IN-ONE dummies	**Samsung Galaxy S7** dummies	**iPhone** dummies	**Crocheting** dummies	**Nutrition** dummies
9781119251163 USA $24.99 CAN $29.99 UK £17.99	9781119235491 USA $26.99 CAN $31.99 UK £19.99	9781119279952 USA $24.99 CAN $29.99 UK £17.99	9781119283133 USA $24.99 CAN $29.99 UK £17.99	9781119287117 USA $24.99 CAN $29.99 UK £16.99	9781119130246 USA $22.99 CAN $27.99 UK £16.99

PROFESSIONAL DEVELOPMENT

Windows 10 dummies	**AutoCAD** dummies	**Excel 2016** dummies	**QuickBooks 2017** dummies	**macOS Sierra** dummies	**LinkedIn** dummies	**Windows 10** ALL-IN-ONE dummies
9781119311041 USA $24.99 CAN $29.99 UK £17.99	9781119255796 USA $39.99 CAN $47.99 UK £27.99	9781119293439 USA $26.99 CAN $31.99 UK £19.99	9781119281467 USA $26.99 CAN $31.99 UK £19.99	9781119280651 USA $29.99 CAN $35.99 UK £21.99	9781119251132 USA $24.99 CAN $29.99 UK £17.99	9781119310563 USA $34.00 CAN $41.99 UK £24.99
SharePoint 2016 dummies	**Fundamental Analysis** dummies	**Networking** dummies	**Office 2016** dummies	**Office 365** dummies	**Salesforce.com** dummies	**Coding** dummies
9781119181705 USA $29.99 CAN $35.99 UK £21.99	9781119263593 USA $26.99 CAN $31.99 UK £19.99	9781119257769 USA $29.99 CAN $35.99 UK £21.99	9781119293477 USA $26.99 CAN $31.99 UK £19.99	9781119265313 USA $24.99 CAN $29.99 UK £17.99	9781119239314 USA $29.99 CAN $35.99 UK £21.99	9781119293323 USA $29.99 CAN $35.99 UK £21.99

dummies.com

dummies®
A Wiley Brand